THE
HORRIBLE
HISTORY OF THE
WORLD

Terry Deary Illustrated by Martin Brown

■SCHOLASTIC

For Gavin Lang, Jane Slater and the Sales & Marketing team at Scholastic. Thanks for ten years of astonishing Horrible Histories success. Here's to the next ten. TD.

For Sally, for everything. MB.

Scholastic Children's Books,
Euston House, 24 Eversholt Street,
London, NW1 1DB, UK

A division of Scholastic Ltd ·
London ~ New York ~ Toronto ~ Sydney ~ Auckland
Mexico City ~ New Delhi ~ Hong Kong

First published in the UK as *The Wicked History of the World*
by Scholastic Ltd, 2003
This edition published 2007

10 digit ISBN: 1 407 10350 4
13 digit ISBN: 978 1407 10350 1

Printed and bound by Tien Wah Press Pte. Ltd, Malaysia

2 4 6 8 10 9 7 5 3 1

CONTENTS

INTRODUCTION

A very clever man called Georg Wilhelm Friedrich Hegel (1770–1831) once said...

*We learn nothing from history.**

Let's face it – you could be out there doing a million exciting or useful things, but *you* are reading this *Horrible Histories* book when clever Georgie has told you that you'll learn *nothing*!

But what does it matter if you learn nothing? Ever since the first *Horrible Histories* book appeared they have been used for all sorts of things...

| TO PROVE HISTORY TEACHERS WRONG... | TO PESTER PARENTS WITH ENDLESS QUESTIONS AND QUIZZES... | TO DISGUST GRANNIES WITH FOUL FACTS AT THE TEA TABLE... |

KING HAROLD WAS KILLED BY A NORMAN ARROW

IT WAS PROBABLY A SWORD, ACTUALLY

WHAT DID THE AZTECS USE TO CUT OUT THEIR VICTIM'S HEART?

BEFORE ROBESPIERRE WAS GUILLOTINED HIS WOUNDED JAW WAS NEARLY TORN OFF

(*Horrible Histories* have also been used to prop up wobbly tables, block draughts under doors, and been torn up for toilet paper – but we won't go into that.)

* The actual words of people from horrible history are always in *italics* in speech bubbles.

4

So why *are* you reading this book? Because you don't believe clever George? No, because this is NOT a book about 'history', it's a book about 'people' – the most disgusting, evil, cruel and *horrible* creatures on Earth.

And this *Horrible Histories* book is in full glorious colour – the most popular colour in it being blood *red*, of course... Our illustrious illustrator needed so much red paint he used dye from 70,000 crushed cochineal beetles.

Imagine that ... the blood you see splashed across these pages is made from real blood and body bits.

So here you have it: a book written to teach you *nothing*. For you to scream, shudder and vomit over. (Some sick people even find some of these disgusting facts *funny*! But you're not like that, are you?)

But BEWARE ... a famous US president called Abraham Lincoln (1809–1865), who was nearly as clever as Georgie, said...

So watch out!

HORRIBLE HUNTERS

Did you know Archbishop James Usher (1581–1656) explained that according to the Bible: 'History began when God made the world in 4004 BC.' But – sorry, God – Jim Usher was WRONG. Probably. (We'll find out when we die and God will either be a) very angry because we said his Bible told lies or b) laughing her socks off and saying, 'I told you so!' because her Bible was right all along.)

What do most people believe today? They believe that the first humans appeared over two million years ago – but because they couldn't write there was no 'history'. They were 'before history' – 'pre-historic' is the posh word.

And these first humans were brilliant. They survived a violent and wild world with no weapons (until they invented them), no fire (till they sorted it out), no clothes (till they learned how to make them). Awful. On the other hand there were no teachers, no schools, no mobile phones or other horrors we suffer today.

So, how did those prehistoric people survive and get to the top of the animal kingdom?

By being more horrible than anything the world had ever seen.

What a shame they couldn't write a million years ago. The stories they could have told…

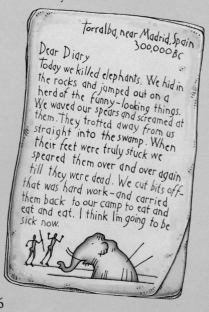

Torralba, near Madrid, Spain
300,000 BC

Dear Diary

Today we killed elephants. We hid in the rocks and jumped out on a herd of the funny-looking things. We waved our spears and screamed at them. They trotted away from us straight into the swamp. When their feet were truly stuck we speared them over and over again till they were dead. We cut bits off – that was hard work – and carried them back to our camp to eat and eat and eat. I think I'm going to be sick now.

6

They may not have had very good weapons but they had invented hunting as a team. People still massacre elephants today – for their ivory, not for food.

In Europe around 70,000 BC a type of human called Neanderthal lived – and they were even uglier than *Horrible Histories* readers!

Some of them had a very nasty habit...

Croatia
70,000 bc

Dear Diary
Today we were hungry. We killed a few of our tribe and cooked them. I enjoyed breaking open the bones to suck the marrow. My dad liked the brains best. They were very tasty, but I will miss the chums I chewed, the buddies I baked and the friends I fried.

The nibbled Neanderthal bones of 20 men, women and children were found at Krapina in Croatia, and bits of Stone Age brain-suckers have been found in Italy. These people had discovered the pleasures of cannibalism and it *still* happens in some parts of the world!

But beware! The nasty Neanderthals became extinct around 30,000 BC. Not very surprising if they went around eating one another. Then modern humans (*Homo sapiens*) became top ape.

Around the same time some humans made a marvellous journey…

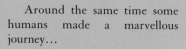

Australia
30,000 BC

Dear Diary
Struth, sport. This arvo we landed on a new land after a huge journey. Animals jumping round like they're on springs.

And cuddly bears that taste great roasted. Will have a barbie on the beach Can't wait to invent beer and cricket.

Humans had invented sea travel and discovered Australia. They became very skilled hunters and survivors – till they were invaded in the 1700s by some simple savages from a country called Britain. But that's another story…

By 20,000 BC, humans had learned to hunt by driving horses off cliffs to kill them – remains of 100,000 horses have been found at the bottom of a cliff in France. That's an awful lot of horse-burgers. But burgers are no good without buns, so five thousand years later…

Nile Valley, Egypt
15,000 BC

Dear Diary
Today Amun took two stones and crushed some corn between them. 'Waste of good corn!' I said. But when he mixed the powder with water and cooked it by the fire he had something very tasty. Wants to call it bread. Who can be bothered with all that baking work, though?

Once humans had bread they learned to grow crops of corn – in the Middle East around 8,000 BC. Now humans didn't have to follow animals around the world to hunt and kill. Now they could stay in one place.

But, about the same time, early humans invented something else very nasty that is still with us...

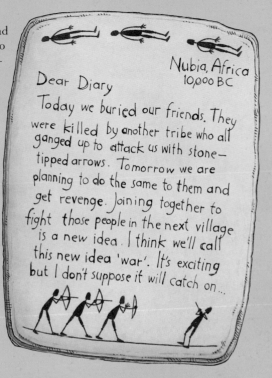

Nubia, Africa
10,000 BC

Dear Diary

Today we buried our friends. They were killed by another tribe who all ganged up to attack us with stone-tipped arrows. Tomorrow we are planning to do the same to them and get revenge. Joining together to fight those people in the next village is a new idea. I think we'll call this new idea 'war'. It's exciting but I don't suppose it will catch on...

DID YOU KNOW...?

OH GREAT ONE, WE ADORE YOU...WITH KETCHUP AND CHIPS

Cavemen worshipped bears – by killing them! They danced around the bear and stuck spears into its lungs. Then they placed its head on a clay model of a bear – and ate the rest.

SAVAGE CITIES

About 6,000 years ago humans decided they liked living together in groups and staying in one place. They began to gather in places with lots of houses – they needed a word for these...

I THINK WE SHOULD CALL IT A 'COMPACTLY-SETTLED-AREA-AS-DISTINGUISHED-FROM-SURROUNDING-RURAL-TERRITORY-BUT-LARGER-THAN-A-VILLAGE-AND-AN-AGGREGATION-OF-HOUSES-RECOGNIZED-AS-A-DISTINCT-PLACE-WITH-A-PLACE-NAME'

NAH! LET'S CALL IT A 'TOWN'–COS IT'S TOWN BELOW US IN THE VALLEY

Then the towns became really huge and they needed a new word...

LET'S CALL IT AN 'IMPORTANT-MUNICIPALITY-OF-DENSELY-POPULATED-URBAN-AREA'

NAA! LET'S CALL IT A 'SITTY'...COS IT'S WHERE I GO WHEN I WANT TO SIT DOWN!

Of course the first cities were dirty, smelly, dangerous and great if you wanted to catch a disease, have your purse pinched or your throat cut. And, amazingly, after 6,000 years they haven't changed much and people still live in them! When will they ever learn?

These ancient cities began to spring up in the Middle East in ancient kingdoms like Mesopotamia, Babylonia and Assyria. And the rest of the world began to copy them.

Some cities, like Troy, are still famous thousands of years after they were flattened and buried. They are remembered because of the stories that have been told about them...

Troy story

Around 1200 BC Prince Paris of Troy stole Queen Helen of Sparta from her husband and started a war that lasted ten years. It grew into a legend. Everyone knows how the Greeks hid inside a wooden horse to get into the city.

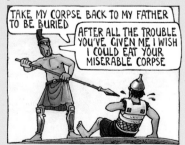

But some of the other nasty bits of the story have been forgotten...

Hero Hector of Troy is speared in the throat by hero Achilles of Greece. As he is dying Hector pleads with Achilles...

Charming. And he drags the body round the walls of Troy behind his chariot.

The Greeks finally enter Troy inside the famous Wooden Horse. Of course the Greeks jumped out and started the slaughter of the Trojans...

The Trojans have a nasty little trick of their own. They take the armour off some dead Greeks and pretend to be Greek soldiers. They get really close to the Greeks and then slaughter them.

In the end the Greeks kill the Trojan men and make slaves of the women. But what about the children? They throw them off the top of the city walls.

11

Kruel kings

Ancient cities might not have been horrible places themselves, but the people who lived in them – and the people who ruled them – could be some of the most horrible humans in history.

Ancient rulers had to be tough to survive. They got to the top by being the biggest bullies – they always had to worry that a bigger bully would throw their big bullying bottoms off their big brassy thrones.

King Sennacherib ruled from 705 to 681 BC in ancient Assyria (northern Iraq and southern Turkey today). He said…

> I CUT MY ENEMIES' THROATS LIKE LAMBS. I CUT OFF THEIR PRECIOUS LIVES LIKE STRING. LIKE THE WATERS OF A STORM I MADE THE JUICES OF THEIR THROATS AND GUTS RUN DOWN ON TO THE WIDE EARTH. MY PRANCING HORSES PLUNGED INTO THE STREAMS OF THEIR BLOOD AS THEY WOULD INTO A RIVER. THE BODIES OF THEIR WARRIORS FILLED THE PLAIN. I TORE OUT THEIR PRIVATE PARTS LIKE THE SEEDS OF CUCUMBERS.

King Ashurbanipal (668–627 BC) followed Sennacherib and was just as nasty. In fact Ashurbanipal's horrors were so disgusting you should *not* read what he wrote about his enemies. To help you *not*

to read about it some of the words are taken out of this terrible tale. Fill them in yourself using your awful imagination. Oh, all right, you can have a few pictures for clues. Ashurbanipal said…

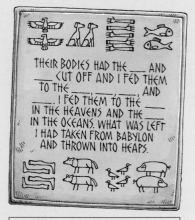

> THEIR BODIES HAD THE ___ AND ___ CUT OFF AND I FED THEM TO THE _____, AND ___. I FED THEM TO THE ___ IN THE HEAVENS AND THE ___ IN THE OCEANS. WHAT WAS LEFT I HAD TAKEN FROM BABYLON AND THROWN INTO HEAPS.

ANSWERS: The missing words in order are: arms, legs, dogs, pigs, wolves, eagles, birds, fish.

Ashurbanipal didn't even let the dead escape his revenge. He said…

> *I broke into the tombs of the old Elamite kings and let in the sun. I carried their bones back to Assyria. I stopped the priests giving them sacrifices so their ghosts were tormented.*

Nice man.

LAW AND DISORDER

Now that people had towns and cities they could gather their precious things in one place. And all sorts of new horrible human things could happen. Now we could have burglary, mugging, fraud and a hundred other new ways of being wicked. So the first laws were invented.

Today we have thousands of laws … and punishments. Some of our punishments are hard to understand – judges send thieves to prison, where they meet other thieves and learn how to be even better villains. But early punishments were easier to understand…

2350 BC Mesopotamia : Urukagina's Code

One of the first great ancient lands was Mesopotamia - Iraq today. And one of their first leaders, Urukagina, left behind 1,200 clay sheets with his laws written on them. Harsh laws...

2050 BC : Ur-Nammu's Code

Ur-Nammu, ruler of Mesopotamia, came up with a new idea...

Sadly Ur-Nammu died in a battle. His war chariot was stuck in the mud and he fell off. An ancient writer said that he was left dying 'like a crushed jug'.

His body was being taken back to Mesopotamia when the boat sank and it was lost...

1700 BC: Hammurabi's Code

Hammurabi of Babylon went back to the cruel old ways. Hammurabi liked to match his punishments to the crimes...

- chopping off hands for a lad who hit his dad
- burning alive for stealing from a burning house
- lopping off an ear for theft
- drowning for charging a customer too much in a pub.

And Hammurabi gave his ideas to the ten most famous laws of all time...

1300 BC: The Ten Commandments

The laws were written down in the Bible and they were fair enough - they said 'Don't kill', 'Don't steal' and so on - but the Bible's punishments were pretty vicious.

These old laws became known as 'An eye for an eye and a tooth for a tooth' - your punishment must match your crime. That can be a bit harsh - if you poke someone in the eye by mistake and have your own eye ripped out!

In 450 BC the Romans went one better than the Bible - no, they went two better, and came up with...

450 BC : The Twelve Tables of Roman Law

Roman laws were not all that fair because the rich got a better deal than the poor. (Ur-Nammu had stopped that nastiness 1,600 years before!) But at least it wasn't a straight 'death for a death' like the Ten Commandments.

Here is a real Roman case. What would you do with the killer?

A MAN WAS BEING SHAVED BY HIS BARBER IN FRONT OF HIS SHOP...
GOING ANYWHERE NICE FOR YOUR HOLIDAYS THIS YEAR?

WHEN A BOY ARRIVED KICKING A BALL...
AND BECKHAMUS SHOOTS AND BECKHAMUS SCORES!

BUT THE BALL HIT THE BARBER'S ARM SO HIS RAZOR SLASHED THE CUSTOMER'S THROAT
NO! HE'S HIT THE BAR BAR

Hammurabi would have had the boy's throat cut, probably – or even the barber's! But Rome was moving away from the savagery of the Stone Age. The judge said...

IT WAS AN ACCIDENT. YOU ARE FREE TO GO

SO, CAN I HAVE MY BALL BACK?

OF COURSE

DID YOU KNOW...?

Alexander the Great (Greek ruler, 336–323 BC) made a rule that said his soldiers could not grow beards. Why?

EEK!
QUITE THE STYLE CRITIC AREN'T WE?

a) Alex was afraid of men with beards after being scared by one as a baby.
b) Alex thought they could be grabbed by an enemy in a fight.
c) Alex had a beard and he wanted to be the only man in Greece with one.

TERRIBLE TOMBS

By 4,000 BC people in Europe were living in shacks made of mud and wood. But their dead families were being buried in beautiful stone tombs. You were better off dead than alive! Deader – but warmer and drier! They were also buried with weapons so they could fight off monsters in the afterlife. Spooky.

Five hundred years later, in Mesopotamia, King Mes-Kalam-Dug went to his grave with enough friends and relations to have a party in the afterlife. They all drank poison and were buried with their king.

But the biggest and best carers for kingly corpses were the Egyptians. Their stone tombs just grew and grew till they became pyramids – the world's biggest stone buildings. Just for a dead king!

By 2620 BC King Djoser's Step Pyramid was built covering 150,000 square metres of desert. That's a lot of sweating workers.

Around 100 years later King Khufu (also known as Cheops) had the Great Pyramid of Giza built.

Writing had been invented by 3200 BC in Mesopotamia. And now we could have written history – and history tests. Great, eh?

But just because the stories from ancient Egypt were written down it doesn't mean they were true! Take the story of King Khufu as told by the Egyptians…

GOOSE MAGIC

Cast: King Khufu Djedi the magician Neria the maid

Scene 1: In the palace

Khufu: Neria, slave!

Neria: Yes, boss?

Khufu: How is my pyramid coming along? It's going to be the greatest pyramid ever built!

Neria: Oh, it's not coming along at all, boss. The workers won't work because you've run out of money to pay them.

Khufu: What am I to do? It's only half finished. There's no point in having a pyramid without a point. I'll be dead soon.

Neria: Tell you what, boss, I've heard about a bloke called Djedi. Says he's a magician who can bring people back to life. He could keep you going long enough to get the pyramid finished.

Khufu: Good thinking. I'm glad I thought of it. Send for Djedi!

Neria: If you ask me he's a bit of a fake. If you ask me he just does tricks.

Khufu: Well, I'm not asking you. Send for him!

Music and stuff as time passes

Scene 2: In the palace – later

Neria: (To Djedi) You're for it, sunshine. The boss wants you to prove you can bring something back to life – or you'll be bringing yourself back to life.

Djedi: I have a goose here in this box. Killed it this morning. (Lifts headless goose out of box.)

Neria: Very tasty. After you've brought it back to life you can kill it again and I'll have it for me supper.

Khufu: Are you the magician?

Djedi: I am Djedi – the greatest magician the world has ever seen.

Khufu: You'll be the richest magician the world has ever seen if you can bring the dead back to life.

Djedi: I have here a goose...

Khufu: Never mind the goose. Neria – I want you to go to the prison and fetch me a prisoner. We'll kill him and let Djedi here bring him back to life!

Djedi: (Panic) You can't do that! No! You can't! It's against the law. Just let me show you what I can do with this goose!

Khufu: Oh, go on then. A bit boring, but go on.

Djedi: (Puts goose in box and closes lid. Waves hands over box then pulls out live goose.) There you are, Your Highness!

Khufu: Great stuff. Come back when I'm dead and do the same for me. I will reward you with riches beyond your dreams. (Khufu leaves.)

Neria: He nearly caught you there, sunshine!

Djedi: What do you mean?

Neria: I mean the live goose was in the box all the time. You just switched it when you put the dead one back in the box. I'm not stupid like the king, you know. He'll have you executed if he ever finds out.

Djedi: You won't tell him!

Neria: I might ... unless...

Djedi: What? What do you want? What is the price of your silence?

Neria: That dead goose for me supper.

Djedi: It's a deal.

Pharaoh phoul phacts

The Egyptian people had been around for such a long time they said the ancient Greeks were 'just children'. The Egyptians were a great nation with great kings called Pharaohs, but here are a few phoul and phunny phacts about them that you don't usually learn in school…

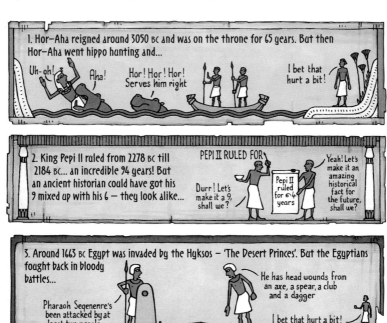

1. Hor–Aha reigned around 3050 BC and was on the throne for 65 years. But then Hor–Aha went hippo hunting and…

Uh–oh!

Aha!

Hor! Hor! Hor! Serves him right

I bet that hurt a bit!

2. King Pepi II ruled from 2278 BC till 2184 BC… an incredible 94 years! But an ancient historian could have got his 9 mixed up with his 6 – they look alike…

Durr! Let's make it a 9, shall we?

PEPI II RULED FOR

Pepi II ruled for 64 years

Yeah! Let's make it an amazing historical fact for the future, shall we?

3. Around 1663 BC Egypt was invaded by the Hyksos – 'The Desert Princes'. But the Egyptians fought back in bloody battles…

Pharaoh Seqenenre's been attacked by at least two people

He has head wounds from an axe, a spear, a club and a dagger

I bet that hurt a bit!

4. Amenhotep III (1386–1349 BC) defeated a rebellion in Nubia. They reckon he killed 312 people in an hour of fighting… and took home the right hands of his victims.

You lie down for a nap and wake up to find they've nicked your hand

It's not right

I bet that hurt a bit!

5. Pharaoh Seti (1291–1278 BC) used Hebrew people as slaves. They begged to be set free but he refused... So Hebrew leader Moses called for God to send disasters to Egypt...

Rivers running with blood!

Probably red algae actually

Plagues of frogs, cattle diseases, hail storms

OUCH

And boils on the bum

I bet that hurt a bit!

6. Moses led the Hebrews to freedom when God made a path through the 'Red' Sea... But actually it was the REED Sea — a shallow lake. An east wind made a dry path for them to cross. And the wind dropped as the Egyptians chased the Hebrews — it drowned them!

Glug, glug!

I bet that wet a bit!

7. One of the greatest kings of Egypt was Rameses II, who died in 1212 BC. Then the mammy–makers tried a new trick to keep his nose in shape under the bandages...

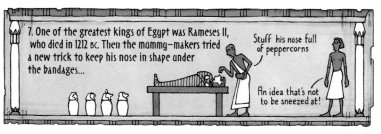

Stuff his nose full of peppercorns

An idea that's not to be sneezed at!

8. In the 520s BC General Phanes betrayed the Egyptians by switching to the Persian enemy. But Phanes had left his sons behind at the mercy of the Egyptians. The Egyptians showed the lads to Phanes on the battlefield...

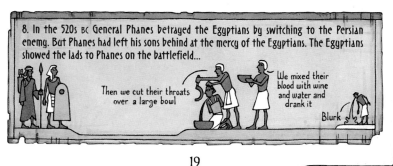

Then we cut their throats over a large bowl

We mixed their blood with wine and water and drank it

Blurk

SUPER SUPERSTITIONS AND QUAINT CUSTOMS

Early humans found the world a mysterious place. They tried to explain it by inventing legends about gods and spirits and performing strange customs. People carried on performing strange customs throughout history. Here are ten of the weirdest – but which are true and which are false?

1. In Jericho (7500s BC), people would cut off the head of their dead grandad, stick it on the floor and worship it.

2. In France (4000s BC), a witch-doctor would cure a headache by beating a patient over the head to scare out the demons in the skull.

3. In Rome (200s BC), the boundaries of a town, village or field were marked with stones. (That's true.) You'd be killed if you moved one of the stones.

4. In India (Middle Ages), when a child is born the mother would have two of her fingers cut off.

5. In Sanghi Islands, Pacific Ocean (Middle Ages), a child would be tortured to death to stop a volcano erupting.

6. In China (1300s BC), priests would get messages from their gods by writing questions on tortoise shells.

7. In France (Dark Ages), Emperor Charlemagne was on the throne for over 400 years.

8. In Italy (1500s), Pope Julius II said, 'God will forgive you anything except murder.'

9. In Scotland (1500s), Mary Queen of Scots would dip a unicorn's horn into her food to test it for poison.

10. In Germany (1940s), Adolf Hitler would melt lead and pour it into water – he thought he could see the future in the shape the lead set in.

ANSWERS

1. True. They filled the old geezer's head with clay, painted the skull to look like flesh and stuck shells in the eye-holes to look like eyes. Then they put it on the floor in the living room – well, they didn't have telly to watch, did they?

2. False. It was much worse. The doc used a sharp flint to drill a hole in the skull and let the evil spirits out. You can't get that from your local doctor today.

3. True. The Romans worshipped the god of boundary stones – Terminus. They decorated his marker stones with flowers and even sacrificed pigs or lambs for the stones. Weird or what?

4. False. But the child's oldest aunt would go to the temple and have two fingers chopped off. She lost the last two fingers on her right hand, which a carpenter would take off with a chisel.

5. True. The village priest killed a kid, cruelly, every year to keep the god of volcanoes happy. First he cut off its fingers, then its nose and its ears and other body bits before finishing it off with a dagger in the chest. The village then had a party for a week – but the kid wasn't invited. Bet he felt a bit cut up about that.

6. True. They wrote a question on a shell (without the tortoise inside) then put a hot iron on the shell till it cracked. The way the shell cracked gave them the answer. They kept a 'library' of shells so they always had the answers to a lot of

questions handy. (They probably ate the tortoises – because fast food hadn't been invented.)

7. True. After Charlemagne had ruled for over 45 years he died in AD 814, but his body was mummified and sat on a royal throne until 1215! He was then buried and is said to be dressed in full armour, waiting to rise from the dead and save the world when it is threatened. Not sure what use a suit of armour will be if the Martians invade!

8. False. Pope Julius II was a crook. He said, 'God will forgive you anything – if you pay me enough money.' The priests of Julius sold 'indulgences' – pardons from God – for any crime. Half the money went to build the Pope's palace in Rome (St Peter's) and the other half went into his greedy, fat pockets.

9. True. Mary Queen of Scots took the 'unicorn's horn' with her from France and used it when she was in prison for 19 years in England. Mary believed it would protect her. She was never poisoned – but the axe on the back of her neck was just as deadly.

10. True. Hitler also believed that the number 7 was lucky. He told his generals to start a new invasion on the 7th of a month – never mind if it was a good time or not. Now you know. Ask your teacher if you can sit your SATs on the 7th for luck and see if it works. (Or, even better – the 77th.)

DID YOU KNOW...?

To change the weather in Japan a dog was often killed with a shower of arrows. A black dog if they wanted rain, a white dog if they wanted fine weather. (Probably shot a Dalmatian if they wanted a spot of rain!)

Lousy legends

Since earliest times people have enjoyed listening to legends. But some legends have been used by people as an excuse for cruel and crafty crimes, like the legend of the Indian goddess Kali…

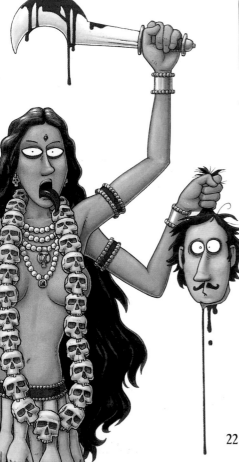

Nasty little story, but harmless enough?

Maybe not. The British ruled India in the 1800s. The Brits *said* the followers of Kali called themselves 'Thuggees' and enjoyed killing for Kali, using white scarves to strangle travellers as sacrifices to the goddess. The Brits *said* they stamped out the cruel custom … but it's possible the Brits made up the whole Thuggee-murderers story so they had an excuse to destoy the Kali religion.

> ### DID YOU KNOW…?
> In India, priests would worship their gods by drinking 'soma' – a drugged drink. But sometimes the drink was made from cow's pee. Cheers!

TOO MUCH COOK MAKES A BROTH

Another legend cost the life of one of the world's greatest explorers...

THE GOD OF HAWAII, LONO, KILLED HIS WIFE AND FELT REALLY SORRY ABOUT THAT. SO HE WENT OFF IN A HUGE CANOE TO WANDER THE OCEANS OF THE WORLD

EVERYONE IN HAWAII WAS SAD TO SEE HIM GO BUT LONO PROMISED TO RETURN TO HIS HAWAIIAN PEOPLE ONE DAY

WE HAVE WAITED A THOUSAND YEARS

Nice story. But it killed the explorer, Captain Cook. How can a story kill a man?

Captain Cook had explored the Pacific for years and discovered Australia and New Zealand. When Captain Cook arrived in Hawaii in 1779 the natives were sure he was their god, Lono, returning just as he'd promised. His ship looked like a huge canoe of the gods.

And Captain Cook let them treat him like a god. Big mistake. When he sailed away a storm damaged his ship and he was forced back to Hawaii.

The natives were shocked! 'How could a god let that happen?' They felt cheated. They killed him ... then they ate him.

Cook's sailors got a bit of his leg and some bones to take home to bury. Cook's head was smashed to a pulp and his bones built into a statue.

COOK?

COOKED!

THE
AWESOME EAST

When most of the world was still in the Stone Age, China had started building an empire. Huang Di was said to be their first great leader around 2697 to 2597 BC. He was known as the Yellow Emperor and was a genius. Today many Chinese people like to believe they are descended from Huang Di and they say all these things about him are true – you make up your own mind how much you believe...

He invented the cart – wheelie useful idea. He invented the boat – that was plain sailing. He invented a compass that pointed south – useful when his war chariots found themselves in a fog during a battle with Chi You. He had 72 brothers with fierce faces – some had heads of bronze and some had animal bodies with human heads. He invented the word 'emperor' and made the royal colour of China yellow – he was no chicken. He had a palace doorkeeper with the head of a man, the body of a tiger and nine tails. He was killed at the age of 110 when (the old books say): 'The land was shattered and broken up by nine dragons.'

The truth is Huang Di was probably a powerful warlord who conquered his neighbours and made one China.

THAT STUFF ABOUT THE LAND BEING SHATTERED BY DRAGONS WAS A LOAD OF TOSH

Maybe NOT! In April 2002 a report came out of China that could explain the old story…

APRIL 9, 2002 8:00 AM EST

BEIJING (REUTERS) - A 5,000-YEAR-OLD METEORITE HAS BEEN UNEARTHED IN HUANGLING IN NORTH-WESTERN CHINA AND IT MAY EXPLAIN THE LEGENDARY DEATH OF THE MAN KNOWN AS CHINA'S EARLIEST ANCESTOR, THE YELLOW EMPEROR.

THE METEORITE, FOUND NEAR THE TOMB OF THE YELLOW EMPEROR IN THE SHAANXI PROVINCE, MAY LIE BEHIND THE 'SHATTERING OF LAND' THAT ANCIENT RECORDS SAY KILLED CHINA'S FIRST EMPEROR, HUANGDI.

THE DISCOVERY ALSO EXPLAINS A LOCAL LEGEND THAT SAYS 'NINE DRAGONS BROKE UP THE ANCIENT TOWN OF HUANGLING'.

HUANGDI IS SAID TO HAVE REIGNED FROM 2697 TO 2597 B.C. BEFORE A DRAGON CAME AND TOOK HIM BACK TO HEAVEN AT THE AGE OF 110.

SCIENTISTS SAY THE METEORITE DATES BACK 5,000 YEARS.

THE SAMPLE, FOUND BURIED DEEP IN THE GROUND, WAS ONLY 82 CM (32 INCHES) LONG AND 21 CM (8 INCHES) WIDE AND HAD BUMPS, HOLES AND TRACES OF BURNED MATTER, SAID LI YANJUN, A YELLOW EMPEROR RESEARCHER.

HE SAID THE METEORITE COULD HAVE CRASHED ON THE TOP OF THE MOUNTAIN WHERE HUANGDI WAS THEN BURIED.

MANAGERS AT THE TOMB SAID THEY HAD NOT HEARD ABOUT THE DISCOVERY.

The ancient people didn't understand meteorites – they explained the flaming trails of explosive rocks as 'dragons'. So maybe Huang Di WAS killed when the land was shattered. If that's true then maybe the rest is.

BUT THE DOORKEEPER WITH NINE TAILS?

ROTTEN RULERS

Once people got together in towns and cities they also started having rotten rulers. These rulers bullied their way to the top and stayed there by being rotten to the people at the bottom. What do you know about rotten rulers? Could you be a terrible tyrant? Count the number of a), b) or c) answers you get to see what sort of ruler you'd make!

1 The Shang family rule China from 1384 BC. While the Shangs live in fine palaces where should they make the poor live?

a) In fine houses with double-glazing, the world's first wallpaper and china ducks on the wall.

b) In poor, crumbling houses with leaking roofs and no ducks.

c) In pits dug into the ground with a roof over the top – and ducks only when the pit became flooded.

2 Roman Emperor Claudius (AD 41–54) has said, 'My stepson Nero will be emperor after me.' How should Nero's mum make sure Nero gets the throne?

a) Be really, really sweet to Claudius so he doesn't change his mind.

b) Threaten to kick Claudius's pet poodle to death if he changes his mind.

c) Poison Claudius with mushrooms before he has the chance to change his mind.

3 Pomaxathres the Parthian has killed Roman general Crassus in battle in Mesopotamia, 53 BC. How should he treat his dead enemy?

a) Treat him with honour and give him a glorious funeral.

b) Treat him as an enemy soldier and throw him in a mass grave with the other dead Romans.

c) Cut off his head and use it as part of a theatre show at the victory feast.

4 Attila the Hun (AD 434–453) is looking for a wife and falls in love with the holy St Ursula. She turns him down. How should he take it?

a) Be heart-broken, but brave, and leave her showered with presents.

b) Be angry and have her locked away until she changes her mind.

c) Kill her with an arrow and have 11,000 of her followers massacred.

5 King John of England has had a row with the Pope in 1209. One of John's priests refuses to work for John till he has made it up with the Pope. What should John do with the priest?

a) Pay him lots of gold to change his mind.

b) Challenge him to a sword-fight – but give the priests a shorter sword and batter him into hospital.

c) Wrap the priest in a heavy sheet of lead and leave him like that in prison so he slowly starves to death.

26

6 Ivan the Terrible of Russia wants to control the great lords – the 'boyars' – in the 1560s. What should he do to them?
a) Give them a good talking to.
b) Lock them in prison until they agree to do as they are told.
c) Have his special police kill them by drowning or strangling or flogging to death or roasting on a spit or frying in large frying pans.

7 Countess Elizabeth Bathory of Transylvania (1560–1615) wants her women servants to entertain her. How should she do this?
a) Teach them to sing, dance, juggle and walk on a tightrope – all at the same time.
b) Teach them to box till they beat one another to a bloody pulp.
c) Stand them in the castle courtyard and pour water over them on a freezing night so they make pretty ice statues.

8 King Frederick William I of Prussia (1713–1740) has a problem with his son who has run away and doesn't take his life as a prince very seriously. How should he change him?
a) Hit him with a cane in public.
b) Hit him with a cane in public and kick him.
c) Hit him with a cane in public and kick him and chop off his best friend's head while he is forced to watch.

9 King Leopold II of Belgium (1865–1909) wants his African slaves to work. He gives them targets to bring so much ivory and rubber. If they fail to reach the targets what should his men do to them?
a) Pay the workers less money so they go hungry.
b) Beat the workers' wives and children.
c) Cut off the workers' hands.

10 The Russians capture German prisoners in the Second World War, but the Germans capture the son of the Russian leader, Josef Stalin. They offer Stalin a swap – German prisoners for his son. What should Stalin reply?
a) 'Yes, please, send my dear boy home to his loving father.'
b) 'Release my son or I will kill your rotten German prisoners.'
c) 'No thanks. Keep him. If he dies, he dies.'

> ANSWERS:
> Score mostly a) – you are either potty or an alien from the planet Zog. You will *never* make a ruler.
> Score mostly b) – you are about as bright as a 20-watt light bulb. But better than the a) people.
> Score mostly c) – a true *Horrible Histories* reader, intelligent, attractive and twisted. All c) answers are what happened in history.

27

ROTTEN ROME

Ancient Rome was one of the greatest cities the world has ever known. How did that happen? If you know how Rome did it then you could make your school the greatest school in the world! So? What made Rome great? Isn't that the sort of question teachers ask? Well, if they ask you, here are a few answers...

What made the city of Rome great?

Answer: Toilets

When towns grew too large they filled up with human waste - pee and poo. But Rome had two ways to deal with this problem:

1. They built dirty great sewers that washed the waste into the River Tiber then out to sea. The sewers were so big you ~~cold~~ could drive a cartload of hay through them — not that you'd want to!

2. Public toilets. Rome had 144 public toilets in AD 315. They even had jars at the corner of the street where men could pee. Once the jars were full they were taken away and used to wash Roman clothes. That's right — they wash their togas in piddle.

Trust you to come up with an answer like this, Darren. You are an expert on toilets, I suppose, as you spend a lot of your school time skulking in them. But you are correct so I have to give you (9/10)

Firemen

Most old cities were built of wood and straw bricks. Of course they kept burning down. Rome was the same. And the Romans lived in blocks of flats and cooked on open fires. Deadly!

Then along came this posh crook called Crassus. He got 500 slaves and set them up as a fire brigade. If your house caught fire he would say, "I'll buy it off you dead cheap and put the fire out."

If you said "No," then he let it burn down. If you said "Yes," then he added another house to his collection.

After he died the Emperor Augustus set up a fire brigade and had watchmen on duty all day and all night. It didn't stop all the fires — there was a huge one in AD 62 — but it helped.

Very neat handwriting Asif. But did you give this answer because your dad's a fireman and you want to be one when you leave school? (7/10)

Law and order

Old cities were dangerous places. No street lights and lots of muggers. The Romans brought in the army to act as police. And the criminals were given really gory executions. They were taken to the arena and made to fight to the death, like gladiators. And even if they survived, then trained gladiators would come in and finish them off. Sometimes they were thrown to wild bears, crocodiles, panthers or lions.

All this happened while thousands of Romans watched. It was fun for them. It was like watching the ~~telly~~ television only better.

If we had executions like that in this school it would stop bullies like Wayne Crocker picking on me. I would like to have him thrown to the lions.

Sorry Catherine, I don't think there are many lions that would fancy eating Wayne. (5/10)

Bread and circuses   *Juvenal*

At least that's what ~~some Roman~~ said. "All the Roman peasants care about is bread and circuses".

Other cities had riots and rebellions and they wrecked the joint. But the Roman ~~bosses~~ *emperors* made sure the poor people had plenty of free bread. And they also made sure they had plenty of fun and games to keep them out of trouble. They had circuses — not with clowns and things like our circuses, but with rough games like chariot racing. There were four teams — red, white, blue and green — and they all had their own fans. They fought each other like football hooligans in our town. But at least they weren't fighting against the ~~top blokes~~ *city rulers*. Rome was an exciting place to be. Wish our town was that exciting.

It was a violent and cruel place Anika. You would probably NOT enjoy it much.
But good answer (8/10)

390 BC   ~~Gooses~~ Geese

Once upon a time there were some rough men with no clothes. *Gauls* They attacked Rome at night which is dead sneaky. All the Romans were in bed snoring like my dad. But the ~~gooses~~ *geese* heard the rough men coming and they honked their horns and woke up the Romans. If it hadn't been for the ~~gooses~~ *geese* Rome would have been captured and never been great. I likes ~~gooses~~ *geese*. They taste lovely with gravy and roast potatoes.

Good try Julius. You are getting better. Slowly.
(4/10)

29

GRUESOME GAMES

The Romans had the nastiest 'games' in history – killing people for fun while a crowd cheered every drop of blood spilt.

Rich Romans paid to have slaves fight to the death at their funeral. The blood on the grave helped the rich corpse get into Roman heaven. In time the number of fights over the grave grew. If you lived in Rome in 264 BC you'd have seen Junius Brutus Pera's funeral 'games' advertised around the city and on the roads leading in to Rome.

SACRIFICED SLAVES

COME ALONG TO THE WESTERN CEMETERY THIS AFTERNOON AND SEE BLOOD SPILT.

THREE PAIRS OF SLAVES WILL FIGHT TO THE DEATH OVER THE GRAVE OF BRUTUS PERA.

GENEROUS BRUTUS HAS PAID FOR THIS WONDERFUL ENTERTAINMENT. ALL YOU HAVE TO DO IS TURN UP, CHEER AND SAY A FEW PRAYERS FOR THE DEAD MAN. THE SLAVES WILL BE ARMED AND THEY WILL BE FAIR FIGHTS.

BUT ONE OF EACH PAIR WILL DIE...
ONE OF EACH PAIR WILL WIN HIS FREEDOM!
BLOODY GOOD SPORT FOR ALL THE FAMILY!

These gladiator fights grew so large they moved out of graveyards and into arenas. The Colosseum in Rome held 50,000 bloodthirsty Romans. There were thousands of slaves, criminals and animals being slaughtered in the Roman arenas. It all started with funerals – but there were no funerals for the victims – they were usually just thrown into the nearest river. Grim 'games'.

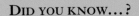

FOWL PLAY

But it wasn't just the Romans who played grim games. Oh no. Take this game from Europe in the Middle Ages, for example...

31

HEN PARTY

'Hunting the hen' was nearly as cruel. For this game (from Europe in the 1700s) you had your hands tied in bandages. You then chased chickens around a yard. The first to pull out a chicken feather was the winner.

In the 1500s, Ivan the Terrible of Russia enjoyed another horrible hen 'sport' with peasant girls...

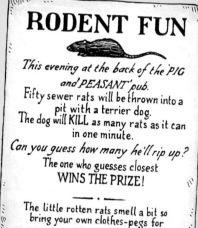

Pick off that Peasant

Tonight at the palace!
Bring your bows and arrows.

Peasant girls will be stripped and set loose to chase five hens... while you shoot at them with bows and arrows! If she catches a hen she goes free... unless you get her first.

Great fun with real moving targets!

ROTTEN RATTING

This sport was popular in Europe in the 1800s but it's probably much older than that...

GONE WITH THE WIND

Here's a sport that was enjoyed by Japanese Samurai warriors in the late Middle Ages. (Don't try this in the classroom. It's much healthier to wait till you get out on to the school playing field.)

RODENT FUN

This evening at the back of the 'PIG and PEASANT' pub.
Fifty sewer rats will be thrown into a pit with a terrier dog.
The dog will KILL as many rats as it can in one minute.
Can you guess how many he'll rip up?
The one who guesses closest
WINS THE PRIZE!

The little rotten rats smell a bit so bring your own clothes-pegs for your noses.

In Ireland a farmer complained that this 'sport' was really popular among the country's priests.

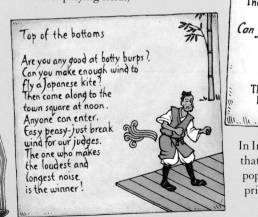

Top of the bottoms

Are you any good at botty burps?
Can you make enough wind to fly a Japanese kite?
Then come along to the town square at noon.
Anyone can enter.
Easy peasy-just break wind for our judges.
The one who makes the loudest and longest noise is the winner!

HOOF HAMMERING

Getting rid of vermin like rats was cruel, but at least the people (and priests) felt they were getting rid of a nuisance. But who would want to see something useful and valuable like a horse battered to death for fun? The Saxons in Northern Germany in the Dark Ages would!

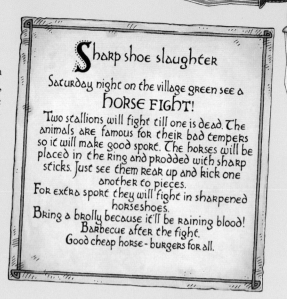

Sharp shoe slaughter

Saturday night on the village green see a

HORSE FIGHT!

Two stallions will fight till one is dead. The animals are famous for their bad tempers so it will make good sport. The horses will be placed in the ring and prodded with sharp sticks. Just see them rear up and kick one another to pieces.

For extra sport they will fight in sharpened horseshoes.

Bring a brolly because it'll be raining blood!

Barbecue after the fight.

Good cheap horse-burgers for all.

33

BEASTLY BARBARIANS

The Romans and Greeks called the people outside their empires 'barbarians' – that's because their speech sounded like 'baa-baa-baa-baa' sounds to the Romans and Greeks. The old history books said these barbarians were rough and ruthless, violent and vicious. But the Romans wrote the history books so they would say that.

Most of the so-called 'barbarians' were just nice lads and lasses trying to make a life for themselves. Now we use barbarian tribe names to put labels on our bad boys and girls – names like 'Vandal'. But were they all that bad?

Horrible historians

Roman historians told the Roman side – usually. But historian Ammianus Marcellinus was better than most. He described one of the worst defeats *ever* suffered by a Roman army and he brings it to life. It happened in Adrianople in AD 378…

The emperor decided to attack the barbarian Visigoths. But such clouds of dust arose that it was impossible to see the sky, which echoed with horrible cries. And so the arrows, which were raining death on every side, reached their mark. They fell with deadly effect, because no one could see them coming through the smoke and dust and no one could guard against them.

The great Roman army wiped out by a dust cloud!

The emperor, Valens, survived the battle but…

Emperor Valens escaped to a nearby farm where he was burned to death by Visigoths. They told him to surrender, his guards answered with a hail of arrows. They set fire to the house and his body was never found. This defeat was the beginning of evils for the Roman Empire then and thereafter.

WHAT DID THEY SAY?

Marcellinus wasn't wrong. The Romans were about to collapse under the barbarian attacks.

The Huns reached the edge of the Roman Empire to the east of the River Rhine. They pushed the Vandal people towards the river and towards Roman lands. But the Vandals couldn't get across – the Romans had a fleet of ships to stop anyone getting over. Yet, in AD 406, the Vandals crossed the wide river at Mainz. They walked across! The river had frozen. The Romans were pushed back, and back and back. It would be the end for the Roman Empire – all because of a freezing night in Germany!

> I COULD DO WITH A FEW WEEKS IN ITALY AFTER THIS

In AD 409 St Jerome wrote a letter about the attack of the Vandals at Mainz...

> I shall say a few words about our present misery. Savage tribes in countless numbers have over-run us. The city of Mainz has been captured and destroyed. Thousands were massacred in its church. The ones who escape the sword die in the famine.

But soon these barbarians were fighting each other. The world was about to head into the 'Dark Ages' with very few historians writing. So it wasn't just horrible historians who told the tales of the Dark Ages, it was also...

Mumbling monks and poets

In the Dark Ages most of the stories were told by monks (who had nothing better to do) and poets (who got paid for it). They told some horrible tales.

The monk Gregory of Tours wrote a history of the Frank (French) people. He told of how the Thuringians (a German tribe) dealt with their Frank prisoners around AD 500...

> *They hung youths by the sinews of their thighs to the trees. They cruelly killed more than 200 girls, tying them by their arms to the necks of horses which were then sent in opposite directions and tore the maidens to pieces.*

Of course the Franks were going to be vicious in their revenge...

> *The Franks killed so many the bed of a river was filled with Thuringian corpses. The Franks stepped on them and crossed the river as if the dead Thuringians were a bridge. The Thuringian king was promised his life would be spared – but the Frank king Theodoric pushed him off a city wall and killed him.*

> TAKE THAT

> EEK!

The Huns were just as bad. Especially the lot led by Attila (AD 434–453). Stories were told of his eating human flesh. But the most gruesome story was that his wife, Gudhrun, served him the hearts of his two sons Erp and Eitil for dinner. She did this because he had murdered her brothers. Poets sang the story for hundreds of years after...

Gudhrun went out to Attila with a golden cup and said, 'Your Highness, you have chewed the bloody hearts of your sons, roasted with honey; you may digest them, brave one! A meal of slain sons, to eat as feast-food. You cannot call for Erp nor Eitil; you shall not see them among the seats giving out gold, smoothing spear-shafts, trimming manes nor driving on horses.' There was uproar among the warriors, there was a furious song, the Huns' children wept, but Gudhrun never cried for her sweet, murdered children.

Mashed monks

The monk Gildas described how the Saxons and Angles from Germany invaded Britain. It sounded a tough old time for the Britons...

The barbarians drive us into the sea. The sea drives us back to the barbarians. Between the two we have a choice: be drowned or slaughtered.

Gildas (who died in AD 570) was writing before the REAL troubles started. That was in AD 793 when the vicious Vikings arrived...

Who did these mighty Viking warriors pick on? The helpless little monks on a North Sea island, Lindisfarne. Were they just bullies picking on helpless men with no weapons? Or did they massacre the monks because they didn't like the way the monks wrote about them? This is what a monk wrote in 'The Anglo-Saxon Chronicle'...

In the year 793 terrible signs appeared in the skies of Northumbria which frightened the people who lived there. Huge flashes of lightning, whirlwinds and dragons were seen flying through the air. A great famine followed soon after. A little later that same year, the attacks of the Vikings miserably destroyed God's church on Lindisfarne with robbery and slaughter.

It was said that the Viking king, Ivar the Boneless, had a nasty new trick – the Blood Eagle torture. Some people say this meant carving an eagle on the back of King Aella of Northumbria when they captured him. Some historians said it meant ripping a victim's lungs out and spreading them across his back like an eagle's wings. Who knows?

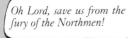

BUT WE ALL AGREE...

...IT HURTS!

Some history writers said the miserable monks came up with a new prayer…

Oh Lord, save us from the fury of the Northmen!

That 'prayer' was first written in 1960 – about 1,000 years after the Viking raids ended! You can't believe everything you read, can you?

Huntastic facts

1. Hun warriors had to eat while they rode to save time. How did they heat up their food? They slipped raw meat between their saddle and their horse's back till it was tasty and warmed by the sweaty horse. (That would be their main course – 'mane' course, see? Horse's mane? Oh, forget it.)

2. The Huns used to cut the faces of their sons when they became teenagers. The scars made them look tough and scary when they went to war. (Don't try this at home. Cut too deep and your chicken and chips will pop out through your cheeks.)

3. The historian Ammianus Marcellinus said the Hun invaders of Rome made their cloaks from the skins of mice! (It would have taken hundreds of herds of mice if the Hun was fat.) But mutt-headed Marce got it WRONG. He was just repeating silly gossip. Never believe everything you read – unless it's in a *Horrible Histories* book, of course.

4. The Huns used to squeeze their children's skulls to make them longer. At birth the baby's head was bound with straps so their soft skulls were squeezed like toothpaste into a bulb at the back. No wonder they were such scary people. But other barbarians copied the Hun head-shapes on their own babies. Why? Because they thought the Huns were wonderful! Great fighters and superstars. They copied their head-shape the way you might copy the hair-style of a pop star or a footballer.

5. The Huns swept towards the Roman Empire on their little horses and could travel 1,500 miles in one week – that's like doing EIGHT marathons every day – when most of us don't do *one* marathon in a *lifetime*! Of course it was the horses that did all the running – no wonder they were small … they probably wore their poor little legs down!

FOUL FIGHTERS

Soldiers through the ages have killed more men, women and children than a million mass murderers – and people don't say, 'You cruel killers!' They say, 'Well done, lads!'

Armies, like schools, have rules. Modern soldiers learn these rules – like you learn school rules! Can you imagine it? Two fighters come face to face and fighting politely?

Today the rules are called the 'Geneva Convention' and were first agreed back in 1864.

GENEVA CONVENTION

Persons taking no active part in the fighting, (including soldiers who have put down their arms and those sick, wounded or taken prisoner) shall be treated well.

1. There shall be NO violence to their life and person, murder of any kind, mutilation, cruelty or torture.

2. The wounded and sick shall be collected and cared for.

Of course people ignore these rules – the way pupils ignore school rules – when they can get away with it! And throughout history wars have been fought with different rules.

So if you want to be a winner, you need to follow the rotten rules on the next page. What are you waiting for? Go out and conquer the world…

THE HORRIBLE HISTORIES
RULES OF WAR

1. The Greeks had strong armies around 675 BC because they fought in tight groups called 'phalanxes'. The trouble was that when the front line fell the second row trampled over the fallen men to get at the enemy.

HH Rule 1: Watch your back. If the enemy doesn't finish you off then your mates will.

2. Attila the Hun used 'terror' as a weapon – people surrendered rather than fight and be horribly tortured if they lost. The Ostrogoth tribe leader Theodoric (AD 454–526) followed Attila but used different methods. He beat his enemy Odovacar at Ravenna in Italy – and entered the city quietly. No terror. He spared Odovacar. Two weeks later he even invited Odovacar to a feast … where he stabbed him to death.

HH Rule 2: Don't trust an enemy who says, 'Let's be friends.'

3. In World War II Adolf Hitler said that women would not have to fight. But by 1944 the Germans were desperate. Women were sent to fire anti-aircraft guns at the British planes. The planes shot and bombed the women, so they ran away. The Germans executed the women for being cowards.

HH Rule 3: Show no mercy to your own soldiers if they let you down.

4. Oda Nobunaga (1534–1582) of Japan was fighting to rule all of the country. While his enemies used swords, Oda used guns he brought in from Europe. Where his enemies had wooden ships, Oda used iron-covered ships. It wasn't an even fight, was it? Like using peashooters to fight machine guns. Of course his iron ships didn't do Oda much good when assassins chopped him down.

HH Rule 4: Give your army the newest, nastiest weapons you can find.

5. Murad IV of Turkey (1612–1640) was potty – but a great success in war. He executed anyone who played a tune that the enemy played. He was a great archer though. He used to practise his aim on any passing woman.

HH Rule 5: Practise your fighting skills on anyone you see.

6. In 1885 in Africa, the Mad Mahdi of Sudan surrounded the British forces in Khartoum and tried to starve them out. When the Mahdi's men finally broke into the city they grabbed the British leader General

Gordon and lopped off his head. Was the Mad Mahdi pleased? No, he was mad … a mad Mad Mahdi in fact. He said that he could have used Gordon to do a deal with the British. His head on a pole was useless!

HH Rule 6: Sometimes a live enemy is better than a dead one.

7. In 1415 Henry V's army of 6,000 English defeated 25,000 French at the Battle of Agincourt. It was the power of the English archers that cut down the French knights — English longbowmen fired up to 20 arrows a minute. The English were cruel – they were afraid their French prisoners would start fighting again, so they killed most of them in cold blood. The French even claimed the English ATE them!

HH Rule 7: Sometimes a dead enemy is better than a live one.

8. Knights in the Middle Ages had rules when they fought each other. But they were not very sporting. If a beaten enemy waved a white flag in surrender you could still beat him to a pulp and knock him out – have a good knight out, you might say. Francisco Lopez, leader of Paraguay (1862– 1870), had wounded enemies thrown into the river to be eaten by passing crocodiles. A snappy way to treat defeated enemies.

HH Rule 8: White flags are for wimps. Ignore them if you want.

9. Spanish knight Rodrigo de Bivar (1040–1099) was known as known as El Cid – The Lord. He dreamt that he would die in 30 days' time – and he did. He ordered his men to fasten his corpse to his war horse when he died so his body could lead his men into war one last time. The enemy saw the mummy riding towards them and ran away. His men won the battle.

HH Rule 9: Don't let a little thing, like being dead, stop you fighting.

10. In 1066 King Harald Hardrada led a vicious Viking attack on England. The Vikings were unbeatable — but his enemy, Harold Godwinson, beat them. How? He attacked the Vikings when they were having a nice little nap. They were dozy, had no weapons and no armour. Like shooting rats in a barrel. Easy peasy.

HH Rule 10: It's easier to murder your enemy in his sleep than in a battle.

NASTY KNIGHTS

Once the Romans had been battered by the barbarians, the barbarians took over their empire. The Franks grabbed the biggest bit of Europe – France. And they had a great idea for grabbing more. Stick soldiers on horses and put armour on them. Then, when they've attacked some enemy armies, these knights can build themselves castles to hide in.

The knights believed there should be 'rules' for their fighting – they called these rules 'chivalry'. We still have them today…

Never mind, there were plenty of people the knights of old *could* hurt – and the Church would bless them for it.

In the Middle Ages, Christian knights found a new enemy: the people who believed in Islam – Muslims. And off the Christian knights went on their 'Crusades' to the Holy Land in the Near East to grab more land and more gold – oh, and to snatch Jerusalem for the Christians (at least that was their excuse). When, in 1099, the Crusaders took Jerusalem they massacred men, women and children.

The Christian knights had a lot to learn from their Muslim enemies. In 1187 the Muslims captured Jerusalem from the Christians. They killed the defenders of the city but there was no mass slaughter.

But all those trips to the East did bring one great treat for the Christians back in Europe – the Black Death. A deadly plague wiped out more than a quarter of the people in Europe.

DID YOU KNOW…?

'Germ warfare' is nasty, because you can't see your enemy; that's why nasty people use it…

- In 1347 a Mongolian army took plague victims and fired them from a catapult into an enemy city, Caffa. They hoped the city people would catch the plague and be easier to defeat.
- In 1758 the British settlers tried to wipe out American Indian tribes by giving them blankets from dead smallpox patients.
- And in 2002 terrorists were sending letters with anthrax germs to their enemies. Time moves on – but *horrible* history returns again and again.

Knight life

Raymond d'Aguiliers went on a Crusade in the 1090s and described the horrors…

DARING D'AGUILIERS DISHES THE DIRT

Handsome Ray relaxing at home (left), with gorgeous views over the countryside (above).

'Once a Knight' (OAK) magazine has a worldwide scoop. We met the famous knight Raymond d'Aguiliers on his return from Palestine and he gave us the very first interview.

OAK: Thanks for talking to us and well done on capturing Jerusalem.

RdA: Thank you, but it wasn't a pleasant job.

OAK: The Crusaders met some fierce fighting?

RdA: Yes and we also met some ordinary men, women and children.

OAK: And spared them?

RdA: No, we massacred them.

OAK: Not very knightly.

RdA: We got a bit carried away.

OAK: So you killed women and children?

RdA: Some of our merciful men cut off their heads.

OAK: And the unmerciful ones?

RdA: Shot them full of arrows or tied them up and threw them onto fires.

OAK: Messy.

RdA: You had to see it to believe it. Piles of heads, hands and feet littered the streets of the city.

OAK: And what about the Muslims who fled to their temple for safety?

RdA: The greatest massacre of all. In the Temple of Solomon men rode their horses in blood up to their knees.

OAK: Guess that's what you would call a real knight-mare!

OAK

Cutter Whey Castle

Some history books show you pictures of what a building might look like if it was 'cut away'. However, at Horrible Histories, the policy has always been to knock down a castle and REALLY cut it away.

We chose to vandalize Cutter Whey Castle in this way. We then invited our artist to draw the ruin and THEN imagine it was full of people as they may have looked in the year 1450.

Our illustrator is fairly good at drawing, as you can see, but happens to be pretty ropy when it comes to history. Our experts spotted TEN mistakes in the picture – ten things that would not be around in 1450.

We did think of sacking the artist and scrapping the painting, then we decided, 'No! Let the Horrible Histories readers see if THEY can spot the mistakes!'

If you think this is too easy then watch out! There are some red herrings – unexpected things which WERE in use in 1450. Well? What are you waiting for?

Score less than 5 and you should go back to a medieval school to be whipped.

Score 5, 6 or 7 and you are not as stupid as you look.

Score 8 or 9 and you are far too intelligent to be doing quizzes like this, show-off. Go back to a medieval school to be whipped.

Score 10? No one will score 10. Answer number 10 is too tricky. If you score 10 then you are almost certainly a cheat and a true *Horrible Histories* reader.

Answers on page 83.

HORRIBLE HEALTH

People in the past were tougher than us. They had to be to survive the foul food, disgusting drink and dreadful disease. Some old cures are still used today – for example, witch hazel plants for sore skin. And acupuncture – an old Chinese idea that sticking needles in you will make you better – is still used for just about everything. (Good excuse if teacher catches you putting a drawing pin on her chair!)

But some cures were just daft or plain disgusting. Here are some from Europe in the Middle Ages…

Teething pain

Baby got sore gums, mum? Don't worry, mum, here's a sure cure for your tot's teeny teeth.

Ingredients:
One large hare

Method:
First catch your hare. Kill it, gut it and skin it. Cut off the head, place the skinned hare into a pot and cook for one hour until tender. Eat it later.

While the hare is cooking take that loppy-eared head and carefully scoop out the brains.

Whisk the brains into a cream and rub the creamed brains into baby's sore gums. If the tot could talk it'd say, 'Yummy, mummy!'

Filthy freckles

Does your child get brown blotches on its face when the sun shines on it? Do friends make fun of its freckles? Banish them now with this cute cure.

Ingredients:
The blood of a hare
The eyes of a swallow

Method:
First catch your hare – use a greyhound to catch it for you. The swallow may be a bit harder to catch because dogs can't fly. Use a net.

Hang up the hare by its feet and cut its throat. Don't forget to put a bowl underneath or you'll make a mess on the floor.

Remove the eyes of the swallow and put them in the bowl with the hare's blood. Grind the eyes till they blend with the blood.

Spread the mixture on the face and leave overnight.

Repeat every spring for freckle-free skin every year.

Scabby skin

Ashamed of your child's blotchy red face? Want to put a paper bag over its head when you have to take it out? Stop that scabby baby now!

Ingredients:
A bulb of garlic
Two spoons of cooking oil

Method:
Place the garlic in a metal bowl and hang it over the fire till it is burned to ashes.

Mix the ashes with the oil.

Spread the mixture over the face of the child. Repeat three times a day and watch those sad sores soar away.

(Note: The child's grey and smelly face may scare its friends for a few days. Keep it indoors till cured.)

Body bending

Those kiddy cures may sound awful but in America the natives liked to change the shape of a baby's head to make it grow up more attractive!

The Incas gave their children pointed heads; the American Indians of Oregon gave them flat heads. How?

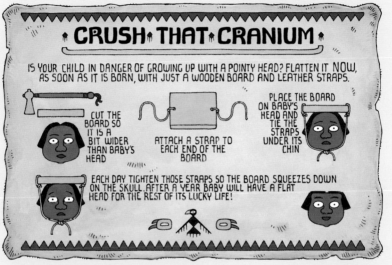

⋆ CRUSH ⋆ THAT ⋆ CRANIUM ⋆

IS YOUR CHILD IN DANGER OF GROWING UP WITH A POINTY HEAD? FLATTEN IT NOW, AS SOON AS IT IS BORN, WITH JUST A WOODEN BOARD AND LEATHER STRAPS.

CUT THE BOARD SO IT IS A BIT WIDER THAN BABY'S HEAD

ATTACH A STRAP TO EACH END OF THE BOARD

PLACE THE BOARD ON BABY'S HEAD AND TIE THE STRAPS UNDER ITS CHIN

EACH DAY TIGHTEN THOSE STRAPS SO THE BOARD SQUEEZES DOWN ON THE SKULL. AFTER A YEAR BABY WILL HAVE A FLAT HEAD FOR THE REST OF ITS LUCKY LIFE!

There was a tribe of American Indians call the Flatheads – but they didn't use this curious custom.

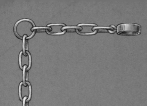

TERRIFYING TORTURE

There have been lots of torturing times in history, but in the Middle Ages, even the Church became a terrible torturer. In Europe around the 1200s, the Church was worried about people who didn't follow their rules – 'heretics' as they called them.

They put them on trial and sentenced the guilty to punishments like: saying some prayers, starving themselves for a few days, handing over their house and land to the church, or going to prison. The ones who refused were often handed over to the government for execution.

Of course, if you're a heretic you might lie to escape your punishment. How could the Church be sure who was telling the truth? In 1252, Pope Innocent IV came up with the answer…

TORTURE THEM

Terrible Torquemada

By the 1480s in Spain, the chief Church torturer was a monk – Tomàs Torquemada, leader of the 'Spanish Inquisition'. The Church let him torture people till they confessed to being a heretic or Jew. But the Church said Tom's torturers must not spill any of their victim's blood. So what did they do?

- Used thumbscrews to squeeze their fingernails.
- Tore their flesh with white-hot irons (to 'seal' the wound before blood could flow).
- Roasted them over fires.

- Forced water down their throats till they almost drowned.
- Hung them from the ceiling by the wrists and put weights on their feet.

But how could you spot someone who may be a heretic, a Jew or a witch?

a) They changed their socks on Sundays.

b) They changed their pants on Sundays.

c) They changed their library books on Sundays.

ANSWER: b) That's right. Anyone changing knickers or underpants on a Sunday could end up in a torture chamber. But how did Torquemada's spies know?

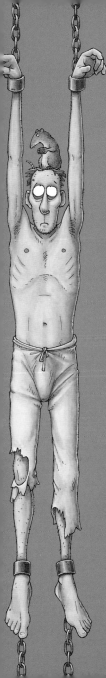

Hus sorry now?

The Catholics had been top Christians for a thousand years but then along came the Protestants. They said silly things like, 'The Catholic Church is too rich. We should be giving more to the poor, just the way Jesus told us to!' The Church said, 'No, we need all our wealth because … er … because we like being rich! Give us more money and we'll make sure God forgives you anything!'

In England it was John Wycliffe (1328–1384) who said, 'We don't need priests.' The priests said, 'You're not putting *us* out of a job, mate.' And they got their way.

But when Jan Hus (1369–1415) said the same thing in Bohemia (Czech Republic) the priests got *very* angry…

Jan's followers, the Hussites, rebelled after his death in 1415. They put cannon on carts and invented a new weapon – a gun on wheels, 500 years before the first tanks were built. It was great for fighting against the Church and its knights. But, like most peasant armies, the Hussites were massacred in the end.

It was left to Martin Luther (1483–1546) in Germany to really lead the Protestants away from the Catholic Church.

What happened to Luther? He set off for a meeting with the Church … and *didn't* die from the heat at the stake. He caught a cold on the journey and died of the chill!

PAINFUL PUNISHMENTS

Animals can kill. But only humans can kill really, *really* slowly so the victim suffers as much as possible. Some torturers in history simply enjoyed seeing people suffer – they did it just for fun, just like boys who pull the wings off flies. Some of their victims must have been happy to die.

SINGED SERVANTS

Elizabeth Bathory, Countess of Transylvania, married Ferenc Nadasdy, 'The Black Hero of Hungary' in 1575 and they started sorting the problem of lazy servants at their castle very soon after…

Varanno Castle
9 May 1575

Dearest Irina

Yesterday we married and today we began to deal with the servant problem. They were so lazy, my dear! Supper was late and the cook said it was because the serving maid was sick. Ferenc sent for the maid and she didn't look very sick to me. We called all the servants into the hall and Ferenc tied the girl to a chair while I fastened each of her ankles to a chair leg. I then dipped slips of paper in oil and slipped them between her toes. I lit the papers and asked her, 'When will you be well enough to start work?'

'Tomorrow,' she whimpered. Then the papers burned down and she felt the heat. 'Tonight!' she squawked. When the flames reached her feet she screamed, 'Now, Now! I'll start work now!'

I turned to the servants and before I blew out the papers I asked, 'Does anyone else feel sick?' Would you believe it, Irina, none of them did?

I think I am going to enjoy being mistress of Varanno Castle.

Your loving friend, Elizabeth

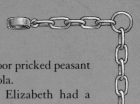

Foul Ferenc liked the 'honey torture'. He captured a peasant and smothered them in honey. The peasant was tied up next to some beehives and the swarming bees stung them to death.

His lovely wife, Elizabeth, believed that human blood could keep her

young. She drained the blood from kidnapped girls and bathed in it. A peasant called Pola tried to run away. She was brought back and shut in a cage full of sharpened blades. They then shook the cage so she was shredded on the points.

Poor pricked peasant Pola.

Elizabeth had a good idea for getting rid of the (empty) bodies. She had them chopped into pieces, went for a drive in her coach and threw a bit out on each leg of the journey. ('Leg' of the journey … geddit? Oh, never mind.)

Elizabeth also tried to get rid of her enemies by having a bath in poison. She would then have the poisonous bathwater stirred into a cake and fed to them. But they didn't die – they just got gut-ache.

DID YOU KNOW…?

• Tsar Ivan the Terrible of Russia had a nasty hobby as a child: he liked to blind dogs and then drop them from a 60-metre tower at the Kremlin palace. He ran down the stairs to watch them die in agony. But he fed his hunting dogs well – he once fed them with Prince Shuisky who was eaten alive by them.

• Ivan's enemy Prince Boris Telupa was spiked on a wooden pole – he took 15 hours to die, talking all the while to his mother who had been forced to watch.

• Ivan carried a wooden pole with a metal spike on to lash out at people who annoyed him. One day he lashed out at his own son and killed him. Deadly sort of dad to have.

CRUEL CHRISTIANS

The Christian Church in the 1500s had one B-I-G rule: 'Believe in Jesus.' Anyone who broke that rule was punished by the Church. One German torturer was keen to use all his torturing equipment on a lady he was trying to save from the Devil's evil clutches...

Germany, 15 November 1597

Dear Dad

Today we had a woman in for saving. She was 69 years old and named Clara Geissler. One of her neighbours accused her of worshipping the Devil. Of course she said that wasn't true. Well, she would. The poor old woman would go straight to Hell if she kept saying that when it was a lie. So we had to get her to admit it, didn't we?

First we put the thumbscrews on her till her fingers bled. Still she said she was a good Christian. But when we stretched her on the rack and used the foot-crusher she owned up. She also named other friends who worshipped the Devil. We arrested them and then started to torture Clara again to check the facts. She died. The priest said, 'Write down that she was strangled by the Devil.'

So, all in all, its been a busy day saving peasants. I hope they are happy in Heaven.

Your loving son,

Heinrich

Of course they would have executed Clara anyway. That was to stop victims changing their minds!

CANADIAN COOKING

A few years later, a French priest went to Canada to preach to the American Indians. They had their own way of dealing with strangers…

IROQUOIS INDIAN CAMP
ST IGNACE VILLAGE
NEAR ONTARIO, CANADA
16 MARCH, 1649

DEAR MOTHER,

TODAY I DRANK THE BLOOD OF A FRENCH CHRISTIAN PRIEST SO I COULD HAVE SOME OF HIS COURAGE. WE CAPTURED FATHER JEAN DE BRÉBEUF BECAUSE HE WAS GOING ON ABOUT HIS GOD AND HIS JESUS. WE DECIDED TO TORTURE THOSE FOOLISH IDEAS OUT OF HIM. FIRST WE STRIPPED HIM AND BOUND HIM TO A POST; WE TORE OUT HIS FINGERNAILS AND BEAT HIM WITH STICKS. HE JUST SAID, 'GOD WILL GIVE ME GLORY'. SO WE POURED BOILING WATER OVER HIS HEAD AND PUT A STRING OF RED-HOT TOMAHAWK HEADS ROUND HIS NECK. WE GAVE HIM A BELT OF WOOD AND SET FIRE TO IT. STILL HE DIDN'T BEG FOR MERCY. HE JUST KEPT TELLING US ABOUT HIS JESUS. TO STOP HIM WE CUT OUT HIS TONGUE AND CUT OFF HIS LIPS – WE SCALPED HIM AND STILL HE LIVED. WE CUT OFF PART OF HIS LEG AND ROASTED IT IN FRONT OF HIM TO EAT IT. AS HE WAS ABOUT TO DIE ONE IROQUOIS CUT OUT HIS HEART AND ATE IT. MAYBE HIS JESUS GOD IS A POWERFUL GOD AFTER ALL?

YOUR LOVING SON

The head of Brébeuf is still kept as a relic at the Hôtel-Dieu, Quebec.

SUPER SACRIFICE

Humans moved into America tens of thousands of years ago. Then they were cut off from the rest of the world and they started to do things differently there. By AD 100 they were sacrificing people differently for a start. Of course the victims ended up just as dead, but the American peoples could make it much more painful!

The Mochica of northern Peru may have been the first American sacrificers – smashing prisoners of war on the head and then drinking their blood. The Maya and then the Aztecs came along later and were probably the most savage people the world has ever seen.

The Maya made human sacrifices complete with…
- tearing out guts
- plucking out fingernails
- death by slow bleeding
- pulling off scalps
- ripping out beating hearts.

It was this last one the Aztecs copied. In 1487 the Aztecs sacrificed 20,000 people in four days. The queues of victims were in four lines, over three kilometres long (almost two miles). Some victims thought it was an honour to be sacrificed. The Spaniards rescued a few victims from the Aztecs and the victims were furious. They *wanted* to die.

HI THERE! TODAY I'M GOING TO SHOW YOU HOW TO SACRIFICE A LUCKY PERSON TO THE SUN. (MAKE SURE THEY'VE HAD A GOOD WASH.)

FIRST WE DRESS THE HAPPY CHAP IN THE SUN GOD'S ROBES, THEN LEAD THE SACRIFICE UP A STEEP STAIRWAY TO THE TOP OF A TOWER ABOUT 30 METRES HIGH

AT THE TOP MY FOUR PRIESTLY FRIENDS EACH GRAB AN ARM OR A LEG AND HOLD THE LUCKY LAD DOWN WHILE I TAKE MY SUPER-SHARP STONE KNIFE

…OF COURSE YOU SHOULD ALWAYS LET AN ADULT DO THIS, KIDS, BECAUSE WE WOULDN'T WANT YOU TO CUT YOURSELVES, WOULD WE?

In the early 1500s the Spanish came across the Aztec people who had enjoyed human sacrifice for hundreds of years.

Bernal Diaz del Castillo, was horrified by what he saw...

They cut off the arms, legs and head then ate the arms and legs at their feasts. They hung up the heads on a wooden beam. The body of the sacrificed man was not eaten but fed to the snakes that guarded their temples. It was so awful I thought I must be in Hell.

Sometimes a priest would skin a victim and wear the skin for 20 days. As the priests never washed their hair or clothes the smell must have been sickening.

NOW I DO THE NEXT BIT VERY QUICKLY SO WATCH CAREFULLY... I RIP OPEN THE CHEST AND PULL OUT THE HEART IN ONE MOVEMENT...

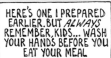

WHILE THAT HEART IS STILL BEATING I HOLD IT UP TO THE SUN

JUST ROLL THAT BODY DOWN THE STEPS FOR THE BUTCHERS TO CARVE UP. WE'LL HAVE A JOLLY GOOD PARTY LATER WITH THAT TASTY MEAT

HERE'S ONE I PREPARED EARLIER. BUT *ALWAYS* REMEMBER, KIDS... WASH YOUR HANDS BEFORE YOU EAT YOUR MEAL

Kruel Killings

The Americans weren't the first to make sacrifices to the gods and they weren't the last. Sacrifice of humans and animals has a horrible history of its own.

1. In the ancient Middle East the Hebrew ruler Jephthah made a deal with God: 'Let me beat the Ammonites in this battle and I'll sacrifice the first thing to walk though the doors to meet me when I get home,' he said. Jephthah won – and the first to walk out to meet him was his only daughter. She was burned alive. Jephthah probably said sorry.

2. In ancient Japan, China, Mesopotamia and Egypt servants would be buried with their dead king. Sometimes the servants were buried alive. This went on until the 1500s in China. In Middle Ages Africa a king's slaves were laid out on the floor of a grave and the king buried on top of them. In Borneo a dead king's slaves were *nailed* to his coffin.

3. In ancient Greece an animal had to agree it could be sacrificed. So the priest said, 'Do you want to be killed?' He then sprinkled water on the beast's head. Usually that made the creature nod its head as if to say, 'Yes, mate, go ahead and give me the chop!'

4. When the Romans arrived in Britain they found Celtic priests called Druids sacrificing animals and humans in a 'wicker man'. A what? It was a huge human-shape made out of wood and packed with straw … and wild animals, cattle and people. The Druids set fire to the straw and stepped back to hear the screams and watch the bonfire. Hot stuff.

5. The Vikings sacrificed cattle at their feasts and ate them. But they also sprinkled the fresh cattle blood over their food before eating it. Yeuch! In Sweden the Vikings sacrificed nine animals of various types every nine years and then hung them up in a wood to rot. The writer Adam of Bremen wrote:

> There are horses and dogs hung there along with men. They do this at the beginning of summer to please the god Odin and hope he will give them victory in the coming battles.

This was in the 1000s when the rest of Europe was Christian and had given up sacrifice.

6. The ancient Chinese had the nasty custom of sacrificing a child to make sure enough rain would fall. They threw a child from a rich family into a deep ditch and drowned it.

7. Early Christians did not believe in sacrifice. (They said Jesus had made the biggest ever sacrifice when he let himself be crucified.) Yet some Christians were still sacrificing animals hundreds of years after Jesus died. Horses were sacrificed to bring luck to:

- dead English King John at his funeral in 1216
- a new monastery in Germany in 1318
- a Methodist chapel in England in 1897. (It was a horse's head that was sprinkled with beer and bricked up into the walls.)

8. In ancient Europe the Celts used human sacrifices to see into the future. The Greek writer Strabo said…

THE CELTS STAB THEIR VICTIM UNDER THE HEART AND THEY SEE THE FUTURE IN THE WAY HE FALLS, THE WAYS HIS ARMS AND LEGS TWITCH AND FROM THE WAY HIS BLOOD SPURTS OUT.

Strabo also claimed the Celts sacrificed people by stabbing them in the back or filling them with arrows.

9. If a Viking died his slave girl could join him in Viking heaven by letting his friends kill her. In Russia in AD 921, an Arab trader watched a Viking ceremony. The slave girl drank a couple of pints of beer, then cried out, 'I see my father and mother. I see my dead relations. I see my master in heaven. Let me go to him!' (If she saw all those dead people it must have been pretty strong beer.) She then started to sing her goodbye song. The trouble is she took so long her killer had to tell her, 'Come on, get on with it!' Charming. Then the girl was strangled and stabbed to death.

10. Tokugawa Ieyasu (1543–1616) is one of Japan's most famous Shoguns (warlords). But he didn't get the job by being a nice guy. The chief of his tribe ordered him to prove he was loyal and said, 'Tokugawa Ieyasu, kill your wife.' Tokugawa Ieyasu obeyed. Then he was told, 'Order your son to kill himself.' Tokugawa Ieyasu obeyed. Would your dad do that to you just to get power?

DID YOU KNOW…?

In India from 100 BC, when a Hindu husband died his body was burned. His widow was expected to throw herself on the fire and die. (This may have been better than slowly starving to death with no husband to earn food for her.) This suicide was called 'suttee' and was made illegal in 1829. 'Sooty' is what the widow ended up.

EVIL
EXPLORERS

Once Christopher Columbus came across America in 1492 there was no stopping the Europeans. They were back and forth like tourists on trips to Torremolinos. But, unlike the Torremolinos tourists, they didn't come to give money to the locals – they came to plunder their gold, sell them as slaves ... and massacre them to extinction if they tried to fight back.

English heroes of the sea, like Sir Francis Drake (1540–1596), had poems written about their lives – and their deaths. The Spanish wrote a poem about Francis Drake (or Frankie Duck as some wicked school pupils call him).

They said Drake was not 'Drake' but 'draco' ... a dragon. Poet Lope de Vega wrote about Draco Drake...

His eyes of blue shone like the light of dawn;
His fiery breath lit up the heavens on high;
His nostrils poured out black and
smoking clouds;
His mouth sent tongues of flame into the sky.

Maybe the Spanish heroes should have had more songs and poems written for them? Time to put that right.

Christopher Columbus
1451–1506

The Italian who discovered America for the King and Queen of Spain. Try singing this hymn to horrible Chris to the tune of 'Rule Britannia'…

Cruel Columbus, Columbus rules the waves;
He turned Arawakan Indians into slaves.
Cruel Columbus had Arawaks in tears;
Chris liked chopping off an Indian's nose
and ears.
Cruel Columbus, his evil knew no bounds;
Slaves who ran away were torn apart
by hounds.
Cruel Columbus, he sailed the seas for Spain.
And the world would never be the same again.

Hernán Cortés 1485–1547

Horrible Hernán landed in Mexico where the dear little Aztecs were ripping out human hearts, eating enemies and generally having a good time. Cortés put a stop to that. The Aztecs believed he was the god Quetzalcoatl and that made it easier for his little Spanish army to defeat them.

Hernán Cortés landed there in fifteen twenty-one,
The Aztecs thought he was a god, just stepped down from the sun.
The Aztec people ripped out hearts and ate their victims' flesh.
Brave Cortés said, 'You must stop that! It makes an awful mesh!'

At that the Aztecs got upset and fought against our hero;
He slaughtered them with sword and gun. His losses? Almost zero.
The Aztecs turned against their leader Montezuma, (king).
They killed him dead with sticks and stones (and other
heavy things).

Cortés said, 'You have a new king – he's the king of Spain!
He wants your gold and silver so cough up!' Oh, what
a pain.
But Cortés had some jealous rivals, they gave him
real strife.
He died a poor old man back home in Spain.
(Ah, well. That's life.)

Actually that's death. But death doesn't rhyme with strife. Sometimes it's hard to be a poet.

EEK!

BOOM!

Francisco Pizarro
1475–1541

In 1531 Francisco set sail for Peru – in search of gold and silver and … you've heard this somewhere before? Frankie was a wrinkly 56-year-old when he set out.

I'M TOLD I'M OLD BUT I'M GONNA BE BOLD AND GET THE GOLD

GOOD GRIEF

He came across the Inca people. Nice people who didn't rip out hearts like the Aztecs. They did have a cute hobby of taking tiny tots on to mountain tops and smashing their heads in as sacrifices. But was that any worse than Frankie Pizarro having the Inca king Atahualpa strangled after paying a king's ransom in gold?

Frankie deserves a good song…

Frankie went off to Peru and grabbed the Inca chief;
'Pay me gold, I'll set you free, you know I'm not a thief.'
Atahualpa (Inca king) paid up on the dot;
Frankie didn't let him go, he pocketed the lot.

Frankie said, 'I hear you've made a plot to do me in.
I am a Spanish Catholic, to me that is a sin.
I will have to burn you!' Atahualpa said, 'Oh, no!
I'll become a Christian too, if you'll just let me go.'

Frankie Piz! Frankie Piz! He's a fighter, he's a whiz!
He made lots of Inca gold, even though he was quite old.

Atahualpa was baptized and Frankie said, 'Well done!
Now you won't be burned up for you've saved yourself, my son.
Go out to the courtyard, lad, we'll save your soul,' he said.
When the king went out the Spanish strangled him quite dead.

You'd think that this would make the Inca warriors quite vexed,
But without their leader they were helpless, all perplexed.
Frankie said, 'Just learn from this and you do what you're told.
I will be your leader – even though I am quite old.'

Frankie Piz! Frankie Piz! He's a fighter, he's a whiz!
He made lots of Inca gold, even though he was quite old.

Frankie made a fortune for his king back home in Spain.
He'd no trouble with the Inca, in Peru he reigned.
No, the trouble Frankie had was with his Spanish friends;
They ganged up on Frankie Piz and chopped him.
That's the end.

Frankie Piz! Frankie Piz! Was a fighter, Was a whiz!
Spanish steel cut him to bits, he died aged sixty-six*.

Yes, Pizarro, like Columbus and Cortés, didn't have as much trouble with the natives as with jealous Spanish friends. Lesson from history? Trust your enemies but don't trust your friends.

* Well, he died on 26 June 1541 and we don't know the exact day of his birth. He *could* have been 65. Does it matter? He was old enough to pick up a pension but had to settle for pushing up daisies.

WOE FOR WOMEN

History is full of famous men. They were most of the rulers and fighters and writers through history. So history is usually HIS-story. Women have often been the horribly unhappy victims...

BEHEADED BOLEYN

The Queen of England from 1533 till 1536, Anne was largely hated by the English people. King Henry VIII made sure she was remembered as wicked even though *he* had poor Anne beheaded. That's how HIS-story can twist things...

 Win a pig! p.17

THE TUDOR TIMES

Friday 19 May 1536

GOGGLE EYES GETS IT IN THE NECK

At 8 a.m. this morning King Henry VIII's ex-wife, the witch Anne Boleyn, died when her head hit the straw at the Tower of London. She had been charged with treason and everyone knew she was guilty.

Ms Boleyn was known for her plain face and her bad temper. As well as her goggle eyes, her mouth was too wide and her skin too dull. The proof that she was a witch lay in the fact that she had six fingers on one hand and a large wart under her chin. Clearly Good King Henry was under one of her spells when he married her!

Today an imported French swordsman took off her head with a single blow. It is said that her heart was stolen from her body to be hidden near her home in Norfolk.

Anne Boleyn going on her 'chopping' trip.

Anne was almost certainly NOT guilty of any crime. Henry was simply annoyed with her for not providing him with any sons. It is said that her ghost can be seen – with her head on her lap – at Blickling Hall in Norfolk.

DROWNING DOLGORUKAYA

Henry VIII also had his fifth wife beheaded. She had another boyfriend and Henry hated that. It seems to be something that really upsets some rulers. Take Ivan the Terrible of Russia and his seventh wife Maria Dolgorukaya ... she only lasted one day!

The Moscow Mail 1574
Kremlin edition

Win a Hat

DIRTY DOLLY DITCHED AND DUNKED!

Wifeless Ivan – Lifeless Maria

Yesterday the Mail reported on the glorious wedding of Tsar Ivan the Awesome to Maria Dolgorukaya. Today we can report her death!

It seems dirty Maria Dolly had had another boyfriend Ivan didn't know about. But when the furious feller found out he had his new bride drowned!

Of course Maria is not the first wife to feel the heat of Ivan's anger. Wife number six, Wassilissa Melentiewna, found herself a new boyfriend – and Ivan found out. The lucky lass was packed off to a nunnery. But not before the bat-brained boyfriend was stuck on a spike and left to die - outside the palace window of Wassilissa!

The Moscow Mail has heard that the next blushing bride will be Maria Nagaya. But how long will number eight last? ∎

In fact, number eight lasted longer than Ivan. Water and spikes were favourite tortures for Ivan. His money manager, Nikita Funikov, was boiled alive. Bet Funikov's wife was not amused...

THAT'S NOT FUNNY!

NO... IT'S FUNIKOV

Chest Look at That!

Women in history have not *always* been 'victims'. Look what happened in the Roman Empire …

AD 95

THE ROMAN TIMES

GLADIATOR OF THE WEEK- IN THE SPORT SECTION | WIN A CELT- SLAVE SECTION | FLAIR WITH FISH GUTS VILLASTYLE SECTION | PART THREE OF OUR DOMITIAN INTERVIEW

ROMANS ROCKED BY WILD WOMEN

Reports are coming in of a Roman defeat on the River Rhine. Our brave boys were beating the Cherusci tribesmen of Germany — as usual — when the Barbarian women suddenly appeared.

The Barbarians use their women as fortune-tellers and listen very seriously to what they tell their fighting men. But this time the Barbarian women didn't just give advice!

Roman historian Tacitus told our reporter what happened next:

'The Germans made a comeback when their women appeared and begged them to fight on. The women lifted up their tunics and showed their warriors their bare chests. They screamed that these lovely bodies would be sent to Rome as slaves if their men didn't fight on. The Cherusci recovered and pushed our soldiers back. They fear the Roman soldiers but even more they fear seeing their women turned into slaves.'

The Roman general in charge was honest about the defeat — you could say he made a clean breast of it. He said, 'I've never seen anything like it!' You can say that again, General!

The Roman Times says, 'Naked women on the battlefield is cheating. Ban them NOW!'

Looks like the Germans came out breast.

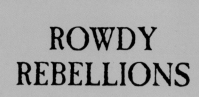

ROWDY REBELLIONS

In the 1600s people were rebelling against their kings and emperors, all over the world. Rebellions to the left, revolutions to the right. Those poor rulers couldn't trust anyone!

In France in 1610 King Henry IV was assassinated – by a monk! If you can't trust a holy man who can you trust? And monks weren't the only ones kings had to look out for. In Bohemia King Ferdinand upset the Protestant people. In 1618, Protestant nobles invaded the palace and threw two of his bodyguards out of the windows. (They landed on a rubbish heap and survived). But body-guarding wasn't all fighting rebels…

In 1622 Turkish Sultan Osman was strangled by his own bodyguards. They led the rebels.

In India the mighty emperor Akbar died in 1605 – he was probably poisoned by his relatives. You couldn't trust anyone.

In England in 1649 the English chopped King Charles I. It was his Parliament that signed his death warrant.

Wicked Waad

In 1605 Guy Fawkes became one of the world's most famous rebels when he failed to blow up both the English MPs *and* their king, James I. Guy was caught.

If you're a ruler how do you stop rebellions? By getting some good torturers to work on the rebs. Guy Fawkes faced the wicked William Waad, Governor of the Tower of London. We know what happened to Guy because a Catholic priest called Father John Gerard survived Waad's torture and lived to tell the tale…

Then we went to the place of torture. We went in a sort of solemn procession, attendants going ahead with lighted candles because the place was underground and very dark, especially around the entrance. It was a place of enormous size and in it were all sorts of racks and other instruments of torture. Some of these they displayed to me and told me I should have to taste every one of them. Then again they asked me if I was willing to answer their questions. 'It is not in my power,' I answered. Throwing myself on my knees I said a prayer or two.

They led me to a great pillar of wood that was one of the supports of this vast crypt. At the top were staples and here they placed my wrists in manacles of iron. They ordered me to mount two or three steps. My arms being fixed above my head they withdrew those steps one by one so that I hung by my hands and arms. The tips of my toes, however, still touched the ground since I was too tall. Since they could not raise me higher they dug away the ground underneath me.

Thus hanging by the wrists they asked me if I was willing to confess. I replied 'I neither can nor will.' But so terrible was the pain that I was scarce able to speak. The worst pain was in my breast and belly, my arms and hands. It seemed to me that all the blood in my body had rushed up to my arms and hands. I was under the impression at the time that the blood actually burst forth from my fingers and at the backs of my hands. This was, however, a mistake.

Gerard hung there for an hour or so after the questioners left. When they saw that he was not going to talk they did a very clever thing. They left him with a jailer who acted really kindly. He wiped the sweat off Gerard's face and pleaded for Gerard to confess because it was causing him (the jailer) so much misery!

When kindness didn't work they tried horror – three or four men gathered in the chamber and talked aloud: 'He'll be crippled all his life … if he lives through it. But he'll have to be tortured daily until he confesses.'

Gerard fainted after an hour, was revived with water and hung up again till he fainted again. This happened about seven or eight times that afternoon. Waad came back again and asked Gerard to confess. Again he refused. Waad stormed off saying, 'Hang there till you rot!'

Brave Gerard resisted three days of this treatment before he used a rope to escape from the Tower.

Guy Fawkes was just as brave and held out for several days. But Waad wasn't going to lose a second prisoner down a rope. Guards made sure there would be no escape for Guy Fawkes.

MURDEROUS MAGIC

People have always believed in 'magic' – invisible forces that can be very useful if only you can control them. Since early times, someone who appeared to make magic work for them was accused of being evil. Those people became known as 'witches', and 'witches' have had to watch out ever since. (After all, the Bible says: 'You should not allow a witch to live.')

THE VOODOO HOODOO

There was a strong belief in witchcraft in Africa in the Middle Ages. When Africans were taken across the Atlantic as slaves they took their belief with them. On the West Indian island of Haiti witchcraft became known as Vodun (or 'voodoo').

Writers and film-makers made up a lot of nonsense about Vodun believers. They said they killed people and drank their blood. All they killed were chickens, goats, sheep and dogs. They believed this brought them good health, good crops or good luck. (Though it wasn't so lucky for the dead dogs and chopped chickens.)

WITCH-FINDERS FOUND OUT

African Zulu chief Shaka (1787–1828) had witch-finders who 'sniffed out' witches. But Shaka didn't trust his witch-finders so he set them a test. He said a witch had smeared blood on his house and he wanted the witch found. In fact Shaka had smeared the blood himself – but the witch-finders uncovered 300 guilty people! Shocked Shaka had the witch-finders clubbed to death ... witch serves them right.

TOAD IN THE BOWL

Do you live in India and need rain to make your crops grow? Then here's a special spell from the Middle Ages.

(This could well be the idea behind this ancient horrible history joke: What turns from green to red at the push of a button? A frog in a liquidizer.)

A spell of rain

You need:
A live frog, a wooden bowl (used for grinding corn), a corn-crushing stone

To make:
1 Collect water from five homes in the village and put it in the bowl.

2 Take your frog and drop it into the water.

3 The women must sing songs about the drought. If you don't know any then try:
I've got rain on the brain
But I've got none in my drain.
Heavy rain, or just some fog,
Bring rain for my little frog.

4 As you sing, use the crushing stone to grind the frog to a pulp.

5 Wait for the rain to start.

BLOOD CURSE

Do you have an enemy you want rid of? Want them to die painfully? Try this curse from 1600s eastern Europe.

A spot of blood

You need:
A black hen, a white stick

To make:
1 Place the black hen on the floor.

2 Use the white stick to batter the hen to death.

3 Keep the blood and smear a drop of it on your enemy.

4 If you cannot get near your enemy take a piece of their clothing and dab it on that.

5 Your enemy will die in horrible pain like the hen.

(Try it today and the *good* news is you won't go to prison for murder because no one would believe the curse could work. The *bad* news is you would go to prison for cruelty to hens — and serve you right too.)

SPELL-ING TEST

Here are eight magic spells from history – but the spells and their uses are scrambled. Can you match them up?

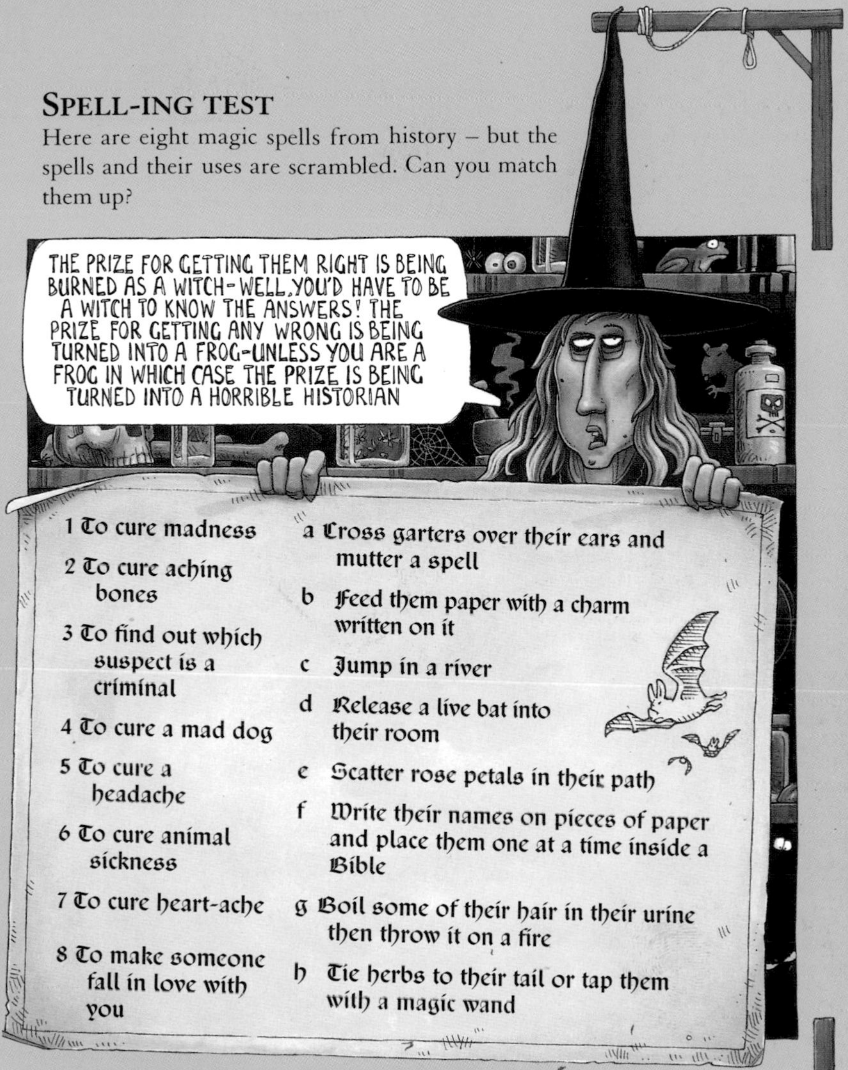

THE PRIZE FOR GETTING THEM RIGHT IS BEING BURNED AS A WITCH–WELL, YOU'D HAVE TO BE A WITCH TO KNOW THE ANSWERS! THE PRIZE FOR GETTING ANY WRONG IS BEING TURNED INTO A FROG–UNLESS YOU ARE A FROG IN WHICH CASE THE PRIZE IS BEING TURNED INTO A HORRIBLE HISTORIAN

1 To cure madness

2 To cure aching bones

3 To find out which suspect is a criminal

4 To cure a mad dog

5 To cure a headache

6 To cure animal sickness

7 To cure heart-ache

8 To make someone fall in love with you

a Cross garters over their ears and mutter a spell

b Feed them paper with a charm written on it

c Jump in a river

d Release a live bat into their room

e Scatter rose petals in their path

f Write their names on pieces of paper and place them one at a time inside a Bible

g Boil some of their hair in their urine then throw it on a fire

h Tie herbs to their tail or tap them with a magic wand

ANSWERS: 1d), 2c), 3f), 4b), 5g), 6h), 7a), 8e). Note: 3f) The Bible will shake when the guilty name is put in.

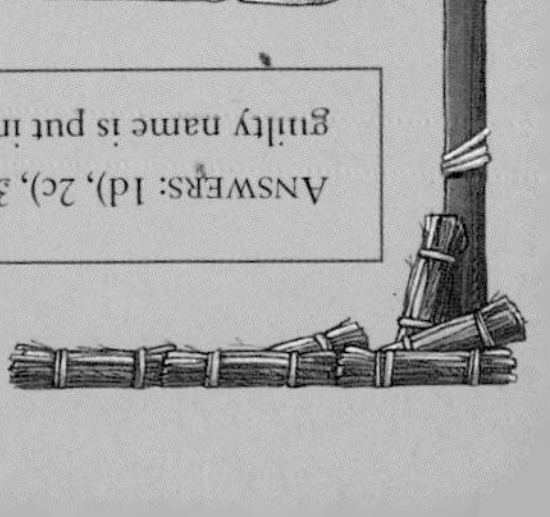

CRUEL CRIMINALS

By the 1700s the people of Europe were roaming the world in their ships. But once they set sail, many of them made their own rules. They robbed others on land and sea, they stole people and sold them as slaves.

Teach's tale

Edward Teach was just one example of the savage 1700s scoundrels…

EDWARD TEACH, BETTER KNOWN AS 'BLACKBEARD', THIS IS YOUR LIFE. BORN IN ENGLAND AROUND 1680 YOU STARTED YOUR SAILING CAREER ATTACKING FRENCH SHIPS.

IT WAS MY JOB. I WAS FIGHTING FOR MY COUNTRY.

BUT, WHEN THE WAR ENDED IN 1716, YOU CARRIED ON SAILING AND ATTACKING SHIPS. THEY RECKONED YOU COULD SPLIT A MAN IN HALF WITH A STROKE OF YOUR CUTLASS. IF YOUR VICTIMS SURRENDERED YOU ROBBED THEM – IF THEY DIDN'T THEN YOU ATTACKED AND MURDERED THEM…

A MAN HAS TO MAKE A LIVING. I HAD A WIFE TO SUPPORT.

IN FACT YOU HAD AT LEAST FOURTEEN WIVES IN BRITAIN AND AMERICA. AND HERE, TONIGHT, IS YOUR LAST WIFE, MARY ORMOND.

I WAS SIXTEEN WHEN YOU MARRIED ME AND I WAS A WIDOW A YEAR LATER. NOT MUCH OF A ROMANCE.

NO, BUT YOU WERE LUCKY, MARY. BLACKBEARD FELL IN LOVE EASILY AND HATED TO BE TURNED DOWN. HERE'S ONE OF THE WOMEN WHO DID TURN HIM DOWN AND CHOSE ANOTHER LOVE … LOOK WHAT HAPPENED TO HER.

I GAVE MY NEW LOVER A RING TO SHOW MY LOVE. BLACKBEARD CAPTURED HIM AND CUT OFF THE HAND WITH THE RING ON. HE SENT THE HAND TO ME IN A BOX. I FAINTED AWAY AND DIED OF A BROKEN HEART.

YOU MAY HAVE BEEN A LADIES' MAN BUT YOUR APPEARANCE TERRIFIED THE MEN YOU MET. EVEN YOUR CREW WERE SCARED OF YOU. COME IN ISRAEL HANDS...

AYE. CAP'N TEACH SHOT ME IN THE KNEE FOR FUN. BEEN CRIPPLED EVER SINCE. HE USED TO PLAIT HIS BLACK BEARD WITH RIBBONS AND TIE SMOKING ROPE TO HIS HAT. OUR VICTIMS THOUGHT THEY WERE BEING ATTACKED BY THE DEVIL HIMSELF.

IN TWO YEARS YOU MADE A FORTUNE BY STEALING BARRELS OF SUGAR AND BALES OF CLOTH. BUT THEY DO SAY YOU HAD REAL TREASURE HIDDEN AWAY SOMEWHERE. BURIED TREASURE.

THE CREW TRIED TO GET YOU TO TELL THEM WHERE IT WAS HIDDEN – IN CASE YOU WERE KILLED. THEY WANTED ME TO HAVE IT. BUT YOU DIED WITHOUT SAYING, YOU BRAIN-DEAD, BLACK-BEARDED BORE!

YOUR LAST BATTLE CAME ON 21 NOVEMBER 1718 WHEN THE BRITISH NAVY IN AMERICA SENT LIEUTENANT ROBERT MAYNARD OUT TO ATTACK YOU. YOU THOUGHT MAYNARD HAD JUST A FEW SAILORS SO YOU JUMPED ON BOARD HIS SHIP...

BUT I HAD A NASTY SURPRISE FOR YOU, TEACH. I HAD A SMALL ARMY HIDING BELOW THE DECKS.

CHEAT!

IN A HAND-TO-HAND BATTLE WITH LIEUTENANT MAYNARD YOU RECEIVED FIVE GUNSHOT WOUNDS AND AT LEAST TWENTY SWORD WOUNDS BEFORE YOU FINALLY FELL.

THAT'S WHEN I CUT OFF HIS UGLY HEAD AND STUCK IT ON THE FRONT OF MY SHIP!

AND THE STORY GOES THAT STILL WASN'T THE END OF YOU. MAYNARD THREW YOUR CORPSE OVER THE SIDE OF THE SHIP, AND WHAT DID IT DO?

SWAM THREE TIMES ROUND THE SHIP BEFORE IT SANK!

AND SO, BLACKBEARD, MURDERER, PIRATE AND BULLY... THAT WAS YOUR LIFE!

SO WHERE'S THE TREASURE?

NOT TELLING!

Tide up and strung up

On land the villains were just as savage. Highwaymen robbed stagecoaches and escaped on fast horses. Laws became more cruel and punishments more deadly but nothing could stop these thugs and outlaws living their brutal lives and dying their violent deaths.

1. Pirates of history became pirates of stories when Stevenson wrote *Treasure Island* in 1881. And when *Peter Pan* was written in 1904 they were made out to be fun, exciting characters. But they weren't! Tales of highwaymen were just as bad. Dick Turpin of England was a vicious murderer – the book *Rookwood* turned him into a sort of daring Robin Hood, and his horse, Black Bess, into a wonderful creature. A folk song, 'Brennan on the Moor', makes the highwaymen Brennan and Dick Turpin sound like heroes…

Oh yeah? Believe that and you'll believe the moon is made of green cheese. (The moon is *not* made of green cheese. *Horrible Histories* researchers have been there and discovered it is made of marzipan.)

2. Pirates could be punished by being hung by their arms to a post in a harbour. When the tide came in – very slowly – they drowned.

YOU'VE HEARD OF LONG JOHN SILVER – THAT WAS *SHORT* JOHN SILVER

3. Pirates DID…
- give an enemy a black spot (or an Ace of Spades) playing card as a sign they were coming to get them.
- wear gold earrings – they believed it helped their eyesight.
- have parrots as pets – they captured them on trips to South America.

A pair of loaded pistols did he carry night and day,
He never robbed a poor man on all the king's highway.
But what he'd taken from the rich,
like Turpin and Black Bess,
He always did divide among the widows in distress.

HOW DO YOU LIKE MY PARROT?

NEEDS A GOLD EARRING ME THINKS

72

4. Pirates did NOT…
- make anyone walk the plank. They threw victims overboard or told them to 'walk home.' But there is no true example of a plank being used.
- always fly a skull and crossbones flag. They flew a black flag which meant 'Stop and we won't harm you.' *Some* pirates had skulls, crossed swords, devils or bleeding hearts on their flags.

5. In the 1700s, pirate Maria Cobham wore the uniform of a navy officer she had killed. She was every bit as cruel as the men. When she wanted to practise pistol shooting it's said she used live sailors as targets. In the early 1800s, Chinese woman pirate Ching Shih had a huge navy of 2,000 boats and 80,000 sailors.

6. Why did highway robbery suddenly become popular in the 1700s? Because the flintlock pistol had been invented. It was light enough to be carried in one hand while the other hand held the horse's reins.

7. Highwaymen who'd been hanged by the neck sometimes had their corpses hung in a metal cage to rot by the side of the road. A lesson to anyone else thinking of robbing on that road.

8. Sometimes judges could be as cruel and crafty as the criminals. Judge Jeffreys of England had over 150 hanged in the 1680s. But there were many more that he *didn't* hang – because they paid him! (He died in the Tower of London, you'll be pleased to hear.)

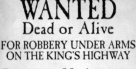

WANTED
Dead or Alive
FOR ROBBERY UNDER ARMS ON THE KING'S HIGHWAY
Dangerous Highwayman
Fitting the following description:
He is a man with fair hair who wears a green coat with gold buttons, grey breeches, high brown turn-down boots with spurs, a white cravat, a blue hair ribbon, an earring and a dark brown hat. He rides a black horse with a white sock on its rear right fetlock. He carries his pistol in his left hand.

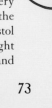

GULP?!

SICKENING SLAVERY

Imagine playing in the fields one day with your kid sisters. Suddenly strangers appear, snatch you and throw you in chains into a dark and filthy, crowded and sweaty ship.

You never see your family again and you will have to work for no wages for the rest of your life – unless you can escape (but then you risk being beaten to death if you are caught).

Imagine losing your freedom and your home and your friends and, what may be worst of all, losing your name!

What would you do? Roll over in the filth of the ship and let yourself die? (The slavers will throw your body over the side so, don't worry, your rotting body won't infect the other slaves and they'll all have a bit more room once you are gone!) Or will you fight and survive?

Olaudah Equiano was captured in 1756 in Africa at the age of 11, and taken to a slave-ship. Here's what he wrote about it...

Olaudah's story

The first thing I saw when I arrived on the coast was the sea, and a slave-ship. These filled me with astonishment, which was soon turned into terror. When I was carried on board I was immediately handled by some of the crew; and I was now sure that I was got into a world of bad spirits, and that they were going to kill me.

Their skin was so different from ours, their long hair, and the language they spoke. I fell lifeless on the deck and fainted.

When I recovered a little, I found some black people about me. They were some of the slavers who brought me on board, and had been receiving their pay; they talked to me in order to cheer me, but all in vain. I asked them if we were not to be eaten by those white men with horrible looks, red faces, and long hair?

I was soon put down under the decks, and there I received such a shock in my nostrils as I had never known in my life; so that with the loathsomeness of the stench, and crying together, I became so sick and low that I was not able to eat, nor had I the least desire to taste any thing.

I now wished for the last friend, Death, to take me; but soon, to my grief, two of the white men offered me food; when I refused to eat, one of them held me tight by the hands, and tied my feet, while the other flogged me.

I had never suffered any thing of this kind before; I would have jumped over the side, but I could not; and, besides, the crew used to watch us very closely who were not chained down to the decks, lest we should leap into the water.

At last, when the ship we were in had got in all her cargo, they made ready with many fearful noises, and we were all put under deck. And the heat of the climate, added to the number in the ship, almost suffocated us.

The air soon became unfit for breathing, and brought on a sickness among the slaves, of which many died. This was made worse by the rubbing of the chains, and the filth of the toilet tubs, into which the children often fell, and were almost drowned.

The shrieks of the women, and the groans of the dying, rendered the whole a scene of horror almost unbelievable.

One day, when we had a smooth sea, two of my tired friends, who were chained together, somehow made it to the side, and jumped into the sea: and I believe many more would soon have done the same if they had not been stopped by the ship's crew. Two of the wretches were drowned, but they got another who tried to follow them, and afterwards flogged him unmercifully, for trying to take death rather than slavery.

At last we came in sight of the island of Barbadoes, at which the whites on board gave a great shout, and made many signs of joy to us.

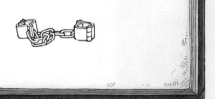

Olaudah Equiano was one of the lucky ones. He wasn't sent to the plantations to be worked to death on the sugar farms. He was bought by a navy captain who changed his name to Gustavus Vassa and took him to England where he learned to read and write. In time he wrote a book about his life which became a great success and helped to get slavery banned. But not before one very curious part of his life...

After fighting in the British navy, Olaudah made enough money to buy his freedom. He became a Christian and returned to the West Indies where he helped to set up a new plantation. And what did Olaudah end up doing?

Buying slaves, of course!

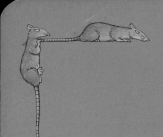

WOEFUL WORKERS

In the 1800s the rich got richer – they built factories to make things faster and cheaper. Of course the workers weren't paid more. They were crammed into filthy houses with no toilets or baths, and drank diseased water.

The British banned slavery from their empire by the 1830s – yet most people working in Britain at that time were little better than slaves themselves.

Look at some of the terrible tasks that some woeful workers had to do…

SWEEPING SLAVERY

Sweeps usually began work about four in the morning – before houses lit their fires for the day. Would you fancy getting up for school at four every morning?

They worked for 12 hours. They'd have probably worked longer but by evening most houses had blazing fires.

The owner of a house was *supposed* to let the fire go cold if they were expecting a sweep – many didn't bother. So the sweeps climbed up chimneys full of hot, choking fumes.

A Manchester sweep described how he trained children…

When you're learning a child you can't be too soft with him; you must use violence… Dozens of sweeps die of lung diseases and they are filthy in their habits. Lads often wear one shirt right on till it's done with.

POP!

There was even a slave trade in boy sweeps. One master sweep reported…

> A boy of about seven or eight was stolen from me once. As he was in the street a man seized him by the arms. He carried the boy off to a lodging house and doped him with drugged tea. An inspector and I traced him to Hull. The thief said that if they had got him on a ship across to France they could have got £10 for him.

MISERABLE MINERS

In the first half of the 1800s, while Queen Victoria was parading in her carriage above ground, girls and women were struggling to make a living by working under the ground. In coal mines.

Women were used to carry the coal from the coal-face to the surface. They would drag the coal in trucks or carry it in baskets on their shoulders. They often had to climb ladders with the heavy baskets on their backs. In 1842 one had to climb so many ladders that end to end she would have reached the top of St Paul's Cathedral …

and she was just 12 years old!

A 37-year-old woman described her work dragging coal trucks…

> I have a belt round my waist and a chain passing between my legs and I go on my hands and feet. The pit is very wet where I work and the water comes over our clog tops always. My clothes are wet through almost all day long.
>
> I have pulled trucks till the belt took the skin off me. The belt and chain is worse when we are expecting a child… My husband has beat me many a time for not being ready on time with the empty tub.

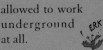

A law passed in 1844 said that children between 8 and 13 years old could work no more than six-and-a-half hours a day. And women were not allowed to work underground at all.

ERK!

COUNTRY COMFORTS

You may think workers had an easier life in the countryside, but the poor lived in awful conditions. The wages for farm workers were terrible and life for a labourer's wife was as bad as anywhere else. A newspaper reporter described his visit to a cottage in 1849…

The wall seems covered in cold sweat and is fast crumbling to decay. It is so low that your face is practically level with the thatched roof as you enter. There are just two rooms, and the only furniture is a small table, three old chairs and a shelf for a few plates. As you enter a woman rises. She is not as old as she looks for she is careworn and sickly. She has an infant in her arms and three other children are rolling on the floor at her feet. They have nothing on their feet and their clothes are rags and patchwork. They are filthy and the woman whines that she has no way of keeping them clean. Two boys and their father have been out at work and they arrive back for dinner. The eldest girl holds the baby while the mother takes a large pot from the fire and pours on to a large dish some potatoes. This with a little bread is their entire meal.

No wonder so many people faced the terrors of exploring the Empire to escape the horrors of 'home' in Britain. (The jungles of India or the deserts of Australia couldn't be much worse.)

DID YOU KNOW…?

In Britain in the early 1800s the average Brit workman would sometimes work up to 96 hours a week for 40p. He survived on bread and butter three times a day. His big treat of the week was the Sunday dinner. Nice chubby chicken or leg of a little lamb? No … half a bullock's head (cost 10p). If you fancy cooking up this delightful dish, you need to skin the head and rinse out the bits of brain. Then boil the head in a pan for two hours. Add a couple of potatoes and onions and cook for another 20 minutes. Yummy.

MMM… I'VE BEEN LOOKING FORWARD TO THIS ALL WEEK

HIDEOUS HOMES

Would you be clever enough to escape the misery of the 1800s? Take a walk down Slum Street: a board game for the bored. Can you make it to the posh houses at the end?

All characters are taken from Edwin Chadwick's report of 1842 into the working people of Britain. All the facts are about Britain – but anywhere in Europe or the USA was just as bad.

Slum Street

You need:

~ Painted peanuts for counters (after all the poor were paid peanuts).
~ Two or more players plus a slave-driver (who will ask the questions – use a teacher or a mugger or a traffic warden or anyone cruel and heartless for this job).

Rules

1

Start your peanuts at the house marked 'Start' and see who can get to the richest house in Slum Street first. To move on to the next house you have to answer the question correctly.

2

All players must declare their answers, then the slave-driver reveals who has got the correct one.

3

The players who get the questions right move up a house. The ones who get it wrong try again next round (when they are bound to get it right, of course, but they'll be behind in the race by then!). If all players get it wrong then they all move up, after reading the answer.

4

If two or more people get to the finish at the same time they share the house and the fortune.

5

The loser should be sent to the nearest coal mine and be made to work there for 16 hours. Well, that's what happened to seven-year-olds in the 1830s so don't say it can't be done. Anyway, you will be paid five pence for your day's work, you lucky loser.

4 Peter Smart's house
'I am forced to work at a water mill. Why?'
a) I am an orphan b) my mother sold me to the mill owner c) I am starving

5 Isabella Read's house
'I am 12 years old. I carry coal underground on my back. How much do I carry at a time?' a) 57 kilos b) 37 kilos c) 17 kilos

6 Sarah Gooder's house
'I am eight years old. I work in the mine and hardly see daylight. What am I frightened of?'
a) the miners b) the pit ponies c) the dark

8 The penniless parent's house
'I couldn't afford to feed my new baby. What have I done with it?'
a) sold it b) sold my furniture to buy it food c) dropped it in the canal

7 James Morrow's house
'I am eight years old and work in the mine. A coal truck crushed my what?'
a) sandwiches b) leg c) head

17 The nail-maker's house
'I make sure my boys work hard and punish them if they don't. How do I punish them?'
a) nail their ears to the work bench b) put salt in their tea c) stand on their toes

18 Benjamin Miller's house
'I am a pit manager. Why do we use women down the mines?'
a) they're cheap b) they're better workers c) they don't complain as much as men

16 The factory overseer's house
'I often get children to work even longer than 19 hours. How?' a) I pay them more b) I take the clock out of the factory c) I beat them with a steel rod

20 Herbert Spencer's house
'I study the workers. I believe...'
a) children should start work at the age of four b) women should not work at all c) weak workers dying is good for the country

19 The factory doctor's house
'I have noticed that the workers are different from other people. How are they different?' a) shorter than average b) pale and ugly c) thin-haired – even the women

The End

ANSWERS

1c) But *only* 14 hours when there wasn't too much work for the factory. They had an hour for lunch.

2b) They did the same knee action hundreds of times a day and their knee stayed twisted.

3a) Workers usually had to guess the time. They were so badly punished for being late they often got there too early before the factory opened.

4b) Parents often 'sold' their children to the factories for as little as 12p a year. If the child tried to run away they were hunted down and taken back.

5a) And Isabella did that up to 30 times a day and up to 500 metres a trip. That's 15 kilometres (9 miles) with the weight of a small woman on your back.

6c) Children had to take their own candles down the mines if they wanted light. Most could not afford it and worked in the scary dark.

7b) James Morrow lost his leg yet went back down the mine with a wooden leg. At the age of nine a rock fall crushed him to death.

8c) A report in the 1860s said 278 children were murdered in London in five years – one a week – by poor parents.

9c) Children dipped sticks in their toilet pits and collected lumps of poo on the end. They wiped the sticks on door knobs of the rich.

10a) Elizabeth was in trouble with the law for fighting Hannah Highfield. The women turned it into a public fight and fought for money.

11c) Isabella had had more children but many died when they were born. She and her husband had worked underground for 30 years. They were 38 years old.

12c) William Shaw's school in Yorkshire was hell for the boys. Charles Dickens wrote the book *Nicholas Nickleby* about Shaw and the teacher was ruined.

13c) Sweeps sent little boys up chimneys. The less they fed them the skinnier the boys stayed and the better they were for climbing chimneys.

14b) Margaret Walters was a 'baby farmer'. She was hanged for letting the

babies in her care starve to death.

15a) Children were also beaten for being even a minute late *and* they lost wages for lateness.

16b) Without a clock the children worked on. Some only got four hours sleep. They got no extra pay.

17a) There were laws to protect children from such cruelty. But the boys didn't dare complain or they'd lose their jobs and starve.

18a) Miller said, 'A man wants three shillings and sixpence (17p) a day but a girl will work for just two shillings (10p) a day.'

19a b & c) Some also suffered twisted spines and flat feet.

20c) Spencer invented the phrase 'Survival of the fittest.' The weak die, the strong get stronger. Result? A country full of strong people. Nasty – but millions believed that … and still do.

CUTTER WHEY CASTLE ANSWERS

Trapdoor Trapdoors weren't used for hanging people until the 1800s. Instead the victim was sent up a ladder and the ladder was taken away.

Fork They used knives, spoons and fingers, but forks weren't used until the 1600s.

Toothbrush Not used in Europe until the 1600s (though the Chinese said they used them as early as 1498). Tooth cleaning was done with a cloth.

Toilet roll Invented in 1871. In the Middle Ages the posh people would use a damp cloth, the peasants would use moss or grass.

Turkey Not seen in Europe until the Spanish came across them in South America in the 1500s.

Horrible Histories First published in 1993. Imagine having to suffer history without those magnificent books! Truly horrible.

Badminton The silly sport of battering a feathered cork wasn't invented till the 1800s … at a place called Badminton. What a coincidence!

Dentist's chair Plenty of people to pull your teeth out with pincers but the special tilting chairs weren't used till the 1800s.

Canned food Not invented till around 1800. Before that food would be steeped in salt to stop it going rotten … or you just ate rotten food and suffered the gut-aches.

Question mark Not invented till 1580s. What do you mean, 'That's cheating'? Oh come on – this is a *Horrible Histories* quiz!

Red herrings: glasses, clock, lighthouse, fireworks, playing cards, pistols, football.

WICKED WARS

The twentieth century was probably the most horrible ever in the history of the world. There were still wars and massacres but now they had wonderful new weapons. Now the killers could kill tens of thousands with the push of a button.

And people could travel by air to attack enemies in their homes. War wasn't about soldiers fighting battles on the 'front line' in some distant country. Now men, women and children could stay at home and be killed by bombs and missiles. Suddenly your house could be the 'front line'.

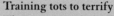

Training tots to terrify

The most evil leaders decided children weren't just there for bomb practice. Today's boys and girls are tomorrow's soldiers. So grab them while they are young. If they are enemy children then exterminate them before they grow to fight you. If they are your own children then train them to hate, kill and obey every order. That's what Adolf Hitler and his Nazi followers did in the Second World War.

In the 1930s the 'Hitler Youth' learned how to be good Nazis. They marched for Hitler through the streets and terrorized the townsfolk. They learned how to fight, and they gave out leaflets for Hitler's Nazi party. They also learned how to cause trouble for other Germans who didn't agree with them!

But they didn't always win. In 1931 and 1932, 21 Hitler Youths died in punch-ups. (No one counted the number *they* killed though!) The Hitler Youth could even ruin adult meetings...

In 1933 Hitler became leader of Germany and the Hitler Youth went from stink bombs to wooden bombs – they had mock battles with the Hitler Youth of other villages. The Germans had lost the First World War (1914–1918). Mr Hitler was preparing for a Second World War and these young warriors would supply his army with ruthless killers.

In 1938 they practised their hatred by helping to attack Jewish people in their homes and burning their synagogues (temples)...

DID YOU KNOW...?

In 1548 at Bodmin School, England, a class of boys were split between those who were for the Catholic religion and those who were for the Protestants. They went to war. One boy turned a candlestick into a gun, loaded it with gunpowder and a stone (for a bullet). He tried it out on a calf – and killed the calf. The boy was whipped by the teacher and the 'war' ended. The calf was probably eaten.

When war came in 1939 there were eight million children in Germany's Hitler Youth ready to fight as soon as they were old enough. Girls trained as defenders, fire-fighters and gunners, too. They had to be tough and marched till their feet blistered...

It was torture for them.

If a girl said she couldn't swim then she was simply thrown into the water. It was

The boys were given other jobs if they were too young to fight. Charming jobs...

I was given the task of walking round the defeated towns of Poland, making lists of the dead and wounded...

I was sixteen. I'd never seen dead people before. Here they were on the ground, dirty and all covered in blood.

As the War went on more and more German soldiers died. Boys took on the job of firing the guns that shot down British and American bombers. They were dressed as soldiers but they were still too young...

The uniforms were too big for us. The underpants came to our armpits and the shirts hung below our knees...

OF COURSE THE ENEMY PLANES ATTACKED US

We were only fifteen – many cried their eyes out.

In 1944 the British and American troops landed in France and began to march towards Germany. That was when the Hitler Youth were thrown into the battles to kill – or die. Only half ever returned to Germany alive.

As Russia attacked from the East the Germans used boys as young as 12 to fight them off...

IF ANY BOYS RAN AWAY THEY SHOT THEM, WE HAD TO WATCH THEM BEING SHOT

AND SOME OF THE HITLER YOUTH WERE THE CRUELLEST FIGHTERS—THEY CARRIED OUT EXECUTIONS OF THEIR OWN PEOPLE

Adolf Hitler was proud of his Hitler Youth boys. Hitler killed himself before the enemy soldiers captured him. He said...

I die with a joyful heart, knowing how bravely our youths have fought, the Hitler Youth who carry my name.

But Hitler was a madman. Years later, one of the Hitler Youth who survived summed things up better...

I was just a frightened child.

DID YOU KNOW...?

In 1945 a Little Boy killed 140,000 Japanese men, women and children in Hiroshima. The Americans dropped a single bomb on the town to end the Second World War. They called the bomb 'Little Boy.' Is that cute? Or is it sick?

MISERABLE MASSACRES

There have always been massacres. Whole groups of people wiped out by the ruthless winners of wars.

Adolf Hitler massacred six million Jews in the 1940s, but he didn't start the idea. Christians had been killing Jews for over a thousand years before. (One of their excuses was that the Jews had killed Jesus – they liked to forget Jesus was a Jew.)

Before the Crusaders decided to kill the enemies of Christ in Palestine they tackled their own home towns. (It was easier killing helpless Jewish families in Europe than Muslim warriors in Palestine.) Albert of Aix saw a massacre take place in Germany. His report, written around 1125, is still chilling.

> At the beginning of summer the Crusaders rose in a spirit of cruelty against the Jewish people scattered through the cities and slaughtered them without mercy. This slaughter of Jews was done first by citizens of Cologne. These suddenly fell upon a small band of Jews and severely wounded and killed many; they destroyed the houses and synagogues of the Jews and divided among themselves a very large amount of money.
>
> When the Jews saw this cruelty, about two hundred, in the silence of the night, began flight by boat to Neuss. The Crusaders discovered them, and after taking away all their possessions, carried out on them similar slaughter, leaving not even one alive.

GOING IN SEINE

Christians didn't just kill Jews or Muslims. They also enjoyed killing other Christians. When Christians divided into Catholics and Protestants in the 1500s they took turns at massacring each other. In some places, five hundred years later, they are still doing it.

In 1572 Catholics in France plotted to kill the Protestant leader Gaspard de Coligny in Paris (and any other poor Protestant Parisians that got in their way). The Catholics dressed with white armbands so they didn't kill each other by mistake!

WITH ALL THIS BLOOD MY WHITE ARMBAND HAS TURNED RED!

ERK!

The Jews of this city, knowing of the slaughter of their friends, fled in hope of safety to Bishop Rothard. They put a large treasure in his guard. Then that excellent Bishop placed the Jews in the very large hall of his own house, so they could stay safe and sound in a very strong place.

But Count Emico - a nobleman, a very mighty man in this region - and the rest of his band held a council and, after sunrise, attacked the Jews in the hall with arrows and lances. Breaking the bolts and doors, they killed the Jews, about seven hundred in number, who could not stop the force and attack of so many thousands.

They killed the women, also, and with their swords pierced tender children of whatever age. The Jews fell upon one another brothers, children, wives and sisters - and thus they died at each other's hands. Horrible to say, mothers cut the throats of babies with knives and stabbed others, wanting them to die by their own hands rather than to be killed by the weapons of the Crusaders.

What was the sign for the Catholics to begin the slaughter?

When the church bells rang. (God must have liked that.)

Gaspard de Coligny's head was sent to the Pope in Rome, it's said, and the Catholics massacred ... er ... depends who you believe! The Catholics *said* they 'only' massacred 2,000 Protestants. The Protestants *said* the Catholics massacred 70,000 of them.

Whoever you believe, a lot of Protestant corpses ended up in the River Seine.

Of course the killers didn't just enjoy the killing, you'll notice. They also enjoyed robbing their victims.

DID YOU KNOW...?

Around AD 440 Attila the Hun's men flattened the city of Naissus (in Yugoslavia). The riverbank was so choked with corpses that the smell stopped people returning to the city for years after. That's what you call a massacre.

Meaningful massacre

Can any good ever come from a massacre? Maybe just once…

In 1859 Henry Dunant was at the Battle of Solferino between the Austrians and the French and Italians. He looked on as 40,000 men lay dead or dying after the battle. There was no one to help the wounded.

Here's Henry's harrowing tale – but will our illustrious illustrator have enough red to paint it?

1 It is a battle of man against man. Both sides trample over one another, striking each other down with the butts of their rifles, shattering the opponent's skull…

2 …slashing open the enemy's stomach with the bayonet or the sabre … there is no mercy.

3 It is a general slaughter, a battle of wild, raging, bloodthirsty animals. Even the wounded defend themselves to the last moment. Those without weapons grab the enemy and tear at his throat with their teeth.

4 It becomes even more horrible when the horse troops arrive at a gallop. The iron hooves of the horses crush the dead and wounded.

(5) One soldier with gaping wounds has his jaw torn away, another his head smashed in.

(6) A third who might have been saved suffers a crushing blow to his chest. The horses' wild neighing mixes with the curses and shrieks of rage, pain and despair.

(7) The horse-drawn guns follow, running over the dead and wounded. Brain matter spurts out of the bursting skulls. Limbs are broken and crushed, bodies torn into formless masses.

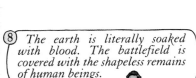

After the battle, Henry set off to create a group of people who would not fight for *any* nation. They would just be there to help any human of any race, any religion or any country. He set up the 'Red Cross' which went on to help millions of victims in the years that followed.

From a horrible piece of history came something good.

Of course, best of all would be for the Red Cross never to be needed. But it has been needed again … and again … and again.

And it will carry on being needed … unless the miseries of war end. Unlikely.

(8) The earth is literally soaked with blood. The battlefield is covered with the shapeless remains of human beings.

EPILOGUE

People have always done horrible things to other people. They did it in cave times and they are still doing it today...

I *TOLD* YOU SO! WE LEARN NOTHING FROM HISTORY!

Don't you just hate it when people say, 'I told you so!'? But you have to admit George Hegel was right.

Humans have mistreated, beated and eated other humans since history began. They are still doing it, somewhere in the world. We learn nothing from history. Humans have attacked, hacked and racked other humans for money, for honey or just because they think it's funny. They are still doing it, somewhere in the world. We learn nothing from history.

On the other hand we hideous humans may be learning something from *horrible* history! Take the Romans. People were crucified, juicified and lions-let-loose-ified in ancient Rome. There isn't a lot of that going on in the world today. Why? Because the Romans got a lot of 'horrible' history written about them. People were *shocked*.

Just as other monstrous people in history have shocked us, from vicious Vikings chopping up harmless old monks to nasty Nazis slaughtering millions of innocent people because they were the wrong race.

When people learn from 'horrible' history then things DO start to change. After the Nazi terrors were defeated, memorials were put up that said simply:

NEVER AGAIN

If George Hegel were alive today he might just have changed what he said to…

So now you know the answer to that question at the start of the book! Why are you reading this book? So you can learn to say, 'Never again.'

The world is still full of horrible happenings. But what will happen in the future to you, young readers?

INTERESTING INDEX

Hang on! This isn't one of your boring old indexes. This is a horrible index. It's the only index in the world where you will find 'body bits', 'horse-burgers', 'scabby skin' and all the other things you really HAVE to know if you want to be a horrible historian. Read it and creep.